COURAGE
and
CONTENTMENT

A Collection of Talks on Spiritual Life
by

GURUMAYI
CHIDVILASANANDA

COURAGE
and
CONTENTMENT

A Collection of Talks on Spiritual Life
by

GURUMAYI
CHIDVILASANANDA

A SIDDHA YOGA® PUBLICATION / PUBLISHED BY SYDA FOUNDATION
www.siddhayoga.org

GURUMAYI CHIDVILASANANDA

Salutations to You from in front and behind,
salutations to You on all sides, O God of All.
You are infinite courage and boundless might.
You pervade all; therefore You are all.

BHAGAVAD GĪTĀ[1]

There is no mantra higher than meditation;
no god higher than the Self;
no worship higher than the inner pursuit;
and no fruit greater than contentment.

KULĀRNAVA TANTRA[2]

Published by SYDA Foundation
PO Box 600, 371 Brickman Rd, South Fallsburg, NY 12779, USA

PHOTO CREDITS
COVER: *Andrei Jewell;* END LEAF: *Joseph De Sciose*
COVER PHOTO: *Mount Kailasa rises in majestic isolation over the austere plains
of western Tibet. Considered the abode of Lord Shiva in the ancient texts of India,
Mount Kailasa has been for centuries the holy destination of pilgrims. Sparkling
with divine power, Lake Manasarovar mirrors the sacred mountain in its waters.*

ACKNOWLEDGMENTS
*Our deepest appreciation goes to all those who contributed their helping hands
and generous hearts to the publication of this volume. For their great dedication and skill, we thank
Valerie Sensabaugh, the managing editor; Patricia Stratton-Orloske and Barbara Yaffe,
who oversaw production; Leesa Stanion for compiling the index;
Cheryl Crawford for the design; Christel Henning for typesetting; and the
SYDA Documentation Department for so carefully preserving Gurumayi's words.*

To each of you, our loving thanks.
Sarah Scott and Kshama Ferrar, editors

Printed in the United States of America
First published 1999

99 00 01 02 03 04 05   5 4 3 2 1

Copyright permissions are on page 156.
Library of Congress Cataloging-in-Publication Data is on page 183.

CONTENTS

INTRODUCTION

COURAGE AND CONTENTMENT—just thinking about these qualities feels good. To face life's challenges with courage, and yet to feel content no matter what happens, surely is the recipe for a useful and happy existence. The question is whether an ordinary person can hope to attain the stalwart inner state needed to live that way. According to Gurumayi Chidvilasananda, the answer clearly is Yes. Gurumayi, the descendent of an ancient lineage of spiritual masters, is a Siddha, firmly grounded in the awareness that only God exists, and capable of awakening others to that same experience. The essence of her teaching is that we can find God within ourselves. As she explains in this remarkable volume, courage and contentment are simply manifestations of the divine perfection that already exists within us all.

The question of how we can be, at once, embodiments of this divine perfection and ordinary people beset with ordinary problems has remained one of the central mysteries of the spiritual quest since time immemorial. Gurumayi is aware, of course, of our struggles with unpaid bills and ringing phones, demanding bosses and frustrating relationships, the ambitions and anxieties that sometimes threaten to drive any thought of divinity from our minds. She sees us as we are, perhaps troubled or uncertain from time to time, but always capable of reaching for the highest.

The gift of a Siddha such as Gurumayi is the ability to awaken us to the recognition of our innermost identity, and then to provide guidance as this potential begins to manifest itself in our lives. The book you are holding now is an opportunity to enter into relationship with a Siddha.

COURAGE AND CONTENTMENT is a collection of talks that Gurumayi delivered during 1996 and 1997. The text reflects her speaking style, which is informal, disarming, welcoming, relaxed—and yet always pointed, always focused on the understanding that she intends to share with us. Readers fortunate enough to have spent time with Gurumayi will appreciate the distinctive personality that enlivens these words and imbues them with the power and intimacy of a face-to-face encounter. Those who have never met Gurumayi will meet her now, for she is fully present in the words that live on these pages.

I first encountered Gurumayi in 1979, when she was serving as translator for Swami Muktananda, the fiery Siddha whose teachings defined the Siddha Yoga path. It was Baba, as we called him, who opened my heart. He initiated me in the unexpected understanding that I could become a yogi, taking a spiritual path even while leading a very worldly life with a wife, two kids, and a hectic career as a business writer and consultant. My early memories of Gurumayi all place her at Baba's side: Modest, attentive, and totally focused, she followed his lead, carefully conveying his meaning into English. She revealed more of her own nature in moments when Baba would startle her by saying something wild and unexpected, shocking her into laughter that showed the depth of her delight in him.

During the past two decades, Gurumayi has emerged as a teacher of extraordinary wisdom and authority, a person possessed of such inner radiance that her presence has the power to spark transformation in others. Gurumayi speaks with a freedom and spontaneity that can provoke laughter and delight. Her penetrating directness readily pierces defenses; her insights have the power to help people change. Like Baba, Gurumayi is simply, totally, real. There is no fluff or pretense in her. She speaks with conviction from a reservoir of personal experience and behaves with a consistency that reflects the rigor and depth of her dedication. Face to face, she can be challenging or tremendous fun, relaxed and playful, without ever losing her focus.

Like Baba, Gurumayi has a way of using words as charged vessels of vast spiritual energy, somehow communicating not just her meaning, but her inner state. That is why thousands of people from all over the world feel grateful for the chance to receive Gurumayi's teachings and her gift of awakening. They are absorbing the state of a Siddha and discovering the riches of their own essential nature.

EVER SINCE I WAS A LITTLE BOY, I've wanted to become a wise old man. For better or worse, I was raised with the notion that the way to manifest strength and courage is to resist all opposition, becoming as fixed and rigid and immovable as a boulder in a raging river. This tough-guy approach has seen me through plenty of challenging situations, from business negotiations to a mugging at gunpoint in New York City. In my middle age, though, I have come to believe that a truer measure of strength and courage is the ability to change and grow as one's understanding expands. As Gurumayi charmingly expresses it, "True steadfastness sparkles with flexibility." Accepting the guidance of a Guru, or spiritual master, was very difficult for me at first. So, for that matter, was the commitment to marry my wife or to write my first book. In all these cases, it was flexibility—the willingness to face facts and evolve—that opened the way to happiness for me. The same principle applies to business organizations: I have often seen how adaptive behavior creates enduring competitive success. During the years when I was coming to appreciate the benefits of change, I was encouraged by Gurumayi, whose example demonstrates what a person can attain. At the same time, my own immersion in meditation was accompanied by a gradual unfolding of courage and contentment in my daily life. So now I can look forward to old age with great optimism: Gurumayi has shown me that the attainment of wisdom is within our reach.

Although honored as a spiritual master, Gurumayi behaves as a model of discipleship. During Baba's lifetime, Gurumayi quite evidently lived to serve her Guru. Now, many years after Baba's passing, Gurumayi rarely speaks for long without invoking his name, acknowledging his grace, making it clear that everything she has become and all that she has accomplished is the gift of her Baba Muktananda. That tender feeling permeates *Courage and Contentment*. The reader becomes aware not only of Gurumayi's love for Baba, but also of her respect for the many other saints and teachers who have revealed the truth of human life over the centuries, from the

Indian king Bhartrihari, to the poet-saint Jnaneshwar Maharaj, to Saint Teresa of Avila.

A DISTINCTIVE ELEMENT of Gurumayi's teaching method is her practice of giving a brief message, or theme, at the beginning of each new year. That message becomes a focus for study, contemplation, and discussion during the whole of the following year, helping students to deeply absorb a particular aspect of yogic thought. During 1997, Gurumayi's theme was *Wake up to your inner courage, and become steeped in divine contentment.* This theme—concerning the nature of courage, the source of contentment, and the power of these two qualities to transform our experience of life—winds and weaves through every chapter of the book. Each talk considers a different aspect of the theme, focusing at times on courage, at others on contentment, elaborating the constant theme by viewing it from fresh perspectives. What the reader receives is less a formal argument than an experience of Gurumayi's state of being. The informality of this approach makes *Courage and Contentment* particularly easy and enjoyable to read. Each chapter is self-contained, yet the impact is cumulative. My practice was to read a chapter at a single sitting and then to set the book aside while Gurumayi's ideas percolated within me; after a few days, I would pick up the book again and read another chapter. The chapters are separated by short passages on the theme from related talks.

One strength of this book is the set of core ideas that informs every chapter. Through her examination of courage and contentment, Gurumayi is exploring the nature of our relationship with God and the impact of that relationship on our experience of life. She starts with the conviction that we are not different from God—that our true identity is divinity itself. We suffer in life because we are afraid, and we are afraid because we have lost the awareness of our union with God. This familiar feeling of separation from what is most worthy, of remoteness from the source of love, wisdom, and peace, inspires misery, dragging us down into the muck of fear and dissatisfaction. The particular alternative that Gurumayi offers is the path of Siddha Yoga meditation, which with grace and practice gives us an inner experience of the divine. This direct, personal experience is what melts away fear, revealing our inherent courage and contentment. Expanding outward into our daily behavior, the virtues of courage and contentment enhance our worldly well-being while quickening the vitality of our inner lives. Courage and contentment are evidence of our union with God; they are also the means to enter into what Gurumayi calls a deeper relationship with our own happiness.

Gurumayi's practicality and good sense make even her more surprising teachings relatively easy to accept. I love her ability to directly engage with the most exalted aspects of human experience, without ever resorting to mumbo-jumbo or pious nonsense. She warns against the temptation to adopt a syrupy smile and spineless acquiescence: "The experience of divine love makes you extremely strong," she insists. "It does not weaken you." Gurumayi urges us not to avoid life's difficulties but to "digest" them, distilling understanding from hardship. Although she strongly emphasizes the need for discipline on the spiritual path, she says we acquire discipline not through brute strength, and not through willpower alone, but through grace. This is the gift she offers. As for us, our principal responsibility is to meditate, steeping ourselves in the knowledge that arises spontaneously from within.

"Contentment," says Gurumayi, "comes when you enter into possession of what you already have." This book is an extended reflection that reveals what we already have. May it bring great joy to us all.

Stratford Sherman
MAY 1999

STRATFORD SHERMAN spent twenty years as a senior journalist at a major U.S. business magazine. An authority on leadership and organizational change, he now divides his time between writing and consulting. He is the coauthor of a best-selling and widely translated book, *Control Your Destiny or Someone Else Will*, a case study about daring and disciplined corporate transformation. Mr. Sherman lives in Connecticut with his wife and two children, and has been practicing Siddha Yoga meditation since 1979.

COURAGE
and
CONTENTMENT

CHAPTER 1

WAKE UP

to your

INNER COURAGE

and become steeped in

DIVINE CONTENTMENT

A MESSAGE FOR THE NEW YEAR

WITH GREAT RESPECT, WITH GREAT LOVE, I welcome you all with all my heart. This is an auspicious moment. We are standing on the cusp of something new and wondrous. Such moments are filled with sparkling possibilities. So let us welcome the time ahead with wisdom, enthusiasm, great affection, and true love. The message we are contemplating is *Wake up to your inner courage and become steeped in divine contentment.*

These two great qualities, courage and contentment, go together. One is born from the other. May you wake up to your inner courage and become steeped in divine contentment. May you wake up to the presence of God within you and savor the bliss of the state beyond desire. May you have the courage to embrace life fully.

Originally, you came to this earth plane knowing there was something you could attain only here and nowhere else. You knew this with absolute certainty. You took birth on this planet, realizing that you have something to offer, something you could accomplish only here and nowhere else. Your being on this planet is a choice you have made. Whether you still agree with it or not, whether you are able to come to terms with it or not, whether things are going well or not, you have made this choice. If you perceive this life as a choice—as *your* choice—it is easier to see how full of amazing wonders it actually is.

To have this enlivening perception, recognize that you have the courage within you to fulfill the purpose of your birth. Summon forth the power of your inner courage and live the life of your dreams. Do you step lightly upon the earth or heavily? On the whole, are the things that come before you full of smiles or frowns? What about your possessions? Do they bring you happiness or unhappiness? Are the people in your life helping you to make greater progress or inhibiting your growth? How much of that is up to you? More than you think! Whether you feel you are winning or losing ultimately depends on the way you approach things and the way you let them approach you.

COURAGE IS NOT JUST A RESPONSE to crisis; it is not just a sudden act of bravery in a fire or a war. And contentment is not merely the sense of satisfaction that comes after you get everything you want. Whatever happens in your life is for your own upliftment. Fragrant, delicious fruit is hidden within every occurrence of every kind. Have the courage to find the best outcome in every situation. Wake up to your inner courage and become steeped in divine contentment.

Whatever the adventures or challenges of life may be, you are the one who has the power to decide how you want to look at things, which way you want to turn your head. Even the best news in the world can bring you down if you insist on it. Your own being in its totality approves or disapproves of your existence on this planet. You hold the reins. You have a choice.

Courage is such a simple word, and yet at the same time it is multifaceted. It holds many other great qualities within itself. Strength, generosity, kindness, hope, love, learning, acceptance of life, and gratitude—these are all a part of courage.

True courage must stem from the depth of your being. It is yours. Courage is the very membrane that shields your heart. Courage is what fends off negativity and transforms adversity into growth. Its undaunted power can pierce through the distracting pull of the senses and make a miracle happen. In fact, courage attracts miracles. Truly, a life of courage is filled with miracles.

IS COURAGE ALWAYS EASY TO FEEL? Easy to spot? Not really. Sometimes courage is invisible. Yet courage is an inherent part of you; it is natural to you. It is really you—*you* are courage. Courage is you. However, just to wake up to the presence of courage inside you takes tremendous courage. It's not like waking up after a nap or a good night's sleep. Waking up to your own courage is actually a matter of waking up to the light of the Truth, to the light of supreme Consciousness within you. An awakening like that demands your firm determination and the touch of grace.

The light of the Truth is infinite. How are you going to actualize it in all its vast magnificence? The best and most efficient thing you can do is to follow one particle, one strand, one ray, of this infinite light. You can follow it by articulating it in language. Then you can begin to discover that the experience of divine Consciousness is within your grasp.

For now, we are following the ray of light emanating from this beautiful and powerful word, *courage. Courage*—what a sweet word. *Courage*—what a strong word. *Courage*— let us follow its light all the way back to its source, to the splendor within the heart.

As the Sufi master Hafiz said:

Come, join the courageous
Who have no choice
But to bet their entire world
That indeed,
Indeed, God is Real.[1]

Wake up to your inner courage and become steeped in divine contentment. Even when you just repeat these words to yourself, "Have courage," you dive into the ocean of your own inner Self and emerge as a new being, dazzling with light. To express the dauntless spirit of inner courage takes a whole new language, and it is good to see this quality in a new light. With this new language and new vision, allow every moment of your life to pulsate with courage and contentment.

THERE IS A FAMOUS CHARACTER called Sheikh Nasruddin. He knew that courage and bravery were very important, and therefore he faithfully attended an annual conference of daring hunters. He loved to go there and listen to people speak about feats of bravery.

One year a hunter stood up and said, "I got hold of the tail of an elephant and twirled him around in the air!"

Another man declared, "I killed a wild tiger with my bare hands."

A third recounted to the group, "With just the power of my gaze, I held an entire pack of rabid hyenas at bay!"

Finally, it was Nasruddin's turn to speak about his most glorious and heroic moments: "Once I pulled out the horn of a wild bull— just like that. Another time I grabbed hold of a huge snake and snapped it into two pieces — just like that. Yet another time I knocked a crocodile unconscious."

"Wow! Wow!" everyone cried. "What else happened, Nasruddin?"

"What else? I had to run for my life!"

"Really? What happened?"

"The owner of the toy shop was coming after me with a stick!"

The courage that we have been empowered with, that we want to discover, is not like Nasruddin's empty boasting. That is the kind of courage some people exhibit when they are merely showing off. They want you to imagine that they are courageous. However, there is real courage within you and you must wake up to it.

WHAT ARE SOME of the other ways that weakness masquerades as courage? Courage is not about breaking the rules to prove to others that you can do exactly what you want. It is not about inviting suffering into your life either, just so everyone can see your unflinching devotion to God. Having courage is not a question of accepting everything that happens passively. To have courage does not mean shrugging your shoulders or sighing, "What can I do? It's my karma."

On the contrary, having courage means engaging in every single situation as a blessing from God, as a loving gesture of nature. Courage means rising to meet the demands of each moment with total delight, knowing you are equal to it. Courage means having faith that within you is an innate force whose essence is never depleted by external events. Live your life courageously, dharmically, knowing that whatever you are faced with is not stronger than you are. You are equal to each other. Your problem is not greater than you are, nor is it smaller. This approach is a dharmic way of living. This is courage. You look at your problem as your equal. And therefore, you can rise to the demands of each moment. With great delight you are able to face and accept whatever comes your way.

EVERYWHERE YOU LOOK, throughout the history of the world, you find wonderful, heartrending stories about courage. You come across stupendous tales and incredible anecdotes. They fill you with the desire to live courageously. They "en-courage" you. What's more, the same sort of events that are written in those tales are also taking place right now. At this very moment there are people who are revealing their vast inner reserves of courage. They are saving the world in both large and small ways. Their benevolent thoughts are full of the light of courage, and this makes their resolutions firm. They have become beacons of courage for others. Right now, all this is happening.

Recognize your inner courage. You have it. You may already be a living hymn to courage. And this is as it should be. The infinite light of the Truth must definitely be translated into everyday life.

I LOVE READING THE BOOKS of my Guru, Swami Muktananda. I love to read his great writings, his wonderful and divine teachings. I turn to them again and again. They are my *prāna*, my life force. His wisdom is my courage. His wisdom is my

life. I continually relish what he has written, what he has given
to us. The messages of great beings are timeless. Their messages are inspired by the infinite light of the Truth, the supreme
Reality, and therefore they always hold something new for
you. Their wisdom resonates completely with your own inner
knowledge, with everything that life has taught you.

However, messages don't come only from the great beings.
A message that calls out to a willing heart can appear anywhere.
For example, you can hear messages even during the simple
conversations and occurrences of daily life. No matter how
casual the words may seem, they can still hold a message of
Truth, of absolute wisdom. Such a message removes the thick
veil from any situation. If you are stuck, a message is a priceless gift that can turn you around.

In every moment, you can find a great message. A playful dog you meet might convey a message of joy and fearlessness that allows you to solve a very difficult problem you are
facing. A weed growing beside the footpath can hold a message. The deep sorrow in the heart of a friend also holds a
message for you. There may be a pebble in your shoe that is
annoying you, yet its presence might hold a message that
wakes you up to your inner courage. The sight of moonlight
streaming through a window may hold a message that
reminds you of the infinite splendor of God. Everyone has
access to this place of blessings; you just have to turn to it and
listen. Listen to the messages that life provides.

NOW, WHAT KIND OF MESSAGES and blessings are you really
seeking? Suppose you are walking down a wintry road and

you are freezing. You know your destination is not far away; however, it is cold. You are losing confidence. The wind is ferocious. Your footing is precarious. The air is so icy it hurts to breathe. And you begin to feel you won't make it. Just then, someone sees you stumbling and invites you into his house. He gives you a hot cup of tea and a warm blanket. This good neighbor rubs your hands and feet to get the circulation going and revives you completely so that you can go on. That is wonderful. Who wouldn't be grateful for such kindness?

But there is a downside to this much needed help. Because if the same thing ever happened to you again, you would be looking for someone to save you. But you might not happen to receive the same loving treatment. You can't always count on being rescued. This kind of help may be a onetime thing.

Now, instead of being offered a hot cup of tea, suppose you come across another sort of help—a person who knows the road and knows how you truly feel. Suppose that friend says, "Have courage. You can do it. Have courage; you are almost there. Look! Your destination is right there!" The warmth of his voice, the certainty emanating from his heart give you the full strength of his blessing. The complete assurance in his voice is like an infusion of energy. The power behind his statement stays with you— "Have courage"— and helps you reach your destination. "You can do it. Have courage; you are almost there."

And when you arrive, what a splendid experience! You have discovered not just your destination: you have discovered your inner courage, and it has brought you to your goal. By waking you up to your inner courage and by giving you faith in your own ability, this true well-wisher gives you a lasting gift. If the same type of incident happens again, you will remember, "Have courage. You can do it! Have courage. You are almost there. Look! Your destination is right there." The message is the lasting gift. You will experience God's blessing, God's grace very strongly. Waking up to your inner courage makes you self-reliant. Once you call on this courage, you recognize it for what it truly is: you see that courage is an exquisite spark of the infinite light of the Truth. And when you call on this divine light, the power of God at the core of your being takes you across. Having courage is invoking God's power within yourself.

Knowing this, Baba constantly urged people to avail themselves of all the strength they carry around inside themselves. He said, "You should have courage, you should have purity, you should have bravery, you should have enthusiasm, and you should have the feeling that you can accomplish everything."[2]

That is the simple truth. Let it fill you with the joy of fearlessness. You can accomplish everything! Wake up to your inner courage and become steeped in divine contentment.

WHAT A MAGNIFICENT FEELING it is to wake up to the presence of your inner courage. To realize that wherever you are, you can actually perceive the brightness of life with your own heart. By waking up to your inner strength, by calling on the virtues of your inner being and putting them into action, you make your heart even stronger. You recognize the divinity that abides in the heart. It does take courage to embrace Baba's teaching: "God dwells within you as you. See God in each other." To understand this fully, you have to wake up. You have to wake up to your inner courage. Someone once told me about a saying: Courage is not the absence of fear but the understanding that other things are more important.

Of all the virtues of spiritual life, courage may be the one that the world finds easiest to recognize. Every nation admires the spirit of courage. As you know very well, the world does not respect cowardice. No one ever wants to extol a person who cringes before the challenges of life or flees from duty. You don't respect yourself either, when you are filled with fear and the desire to quit. Cowardice weakens everything you stand for, everything you believe in. Cowardice has to be one of the worst feelings. Like a deadly poison, it eats away at your mind and spirit, killing you slowly at the very moment you are fighting hardest to survive. It takes courage to strive for the highest. It takes courage to turn your senses within. It takes courage to seek the supreme Self, to seek out the inner worlds. And there-fore, right now, resolve to let every moment of your life be filled with the enthusiasm of courage and divine contentment.

IN THE LIVES OF ALL BEINGS, there is occasion for strife. Does that mean you should give up? Does that mean you should allow your weaknesses to parade around and tell everyone how fee-ble you are? Is that the way God sent you to this earth? No. He prepared you in heaven. He instilled you with courage. He said, "You want to go to the earth because there is something you want to learn there, because you have something to offer there. Go with My full blessing." And how did you feel when you first decided to join everyone on this planet?

Why not think of that moment of courage? You came to this earth with courage. Why do you want to hide it now and go around making people feel sorry for you, making them feel pity for you? Is that the way to serve God? Is that the way to recognize God's presence in everyone?

Cowardice makes everything more painful. It doesn't matter whether you are talking about war, work, or life in general. Cowardice hides behind a veil of false courage and lures you toward destruction. When people are smoldering with anger, resentment, or envy, they say, "If only I had the courage to tell that person what I really think about him!" Can you see how cowardice is hiding behind a veil of false courage here and luring you toward destruction?

What are the other impulses that come up involuntarily when you are in the grip of your emotions? What are the fantasies? When you are stuck in a traffic jam, have you ever wished you could step on the gas and just plow through the cars in front of you? Is that courage? Wishing you were bold enough to tear up all your bills and go to another city and start a new life? Wishing you had the courage to hit the person who makes you so angry?

Foolhardiness and outbursts of anger do not display the kind of courage we are talking about. We are talking about releasing the goodness of your heart. This form of courage is never used as a weapon. It is never called upon to destroy life or to show off.

Where does this courage really come from? Think about it. We are following this ray of light to its source. The scriptures say emphatically that selfish desires involve you in things that deplete you. So courage must arise from somewhere else. It has to come from a place beyond desires, a place where desires starve to death, a place that is rich in wisdom and wholeness.

That place is called contentment: the deep sense of being in the great heart of God, the knowledge of inner fulfillment. Contentment— understanding what is yours and what is not yours, knowing that all of it belongs to God, and resting in this knowledge, taking repose in this wisdom, the supreme peace of the heart.

COURAGE HAS A VERY STRONG relationship with contentment. Not the temporary kind of contentment you experience when you quench your thirst or satisfy your hunger. Not the easy satisfaction of mind that can be bought by soothing words that feed your ego. Not any of the promises of comfort that other people make. Here we are talking about divine contentment in which you experience total surrender. Why? Because you are strong. You surrender not because you are weak; you surrender because you are strong.

As a philosopher once said, "Contentment is a pearl of great price, and whoever procures it at the expense of ten thousand desires makes a wise and a happy purchase."[3]

Between them, courage and contentment bring your world into balance. The poet-saint Akkamahadevi, who lived in India in the twelfth century, once said:

Having been born in this world,
You should not lose your temper at praise or blame,
But maintain the poise of your heart.

Always, Baba Muktananda maintained the poise of the heart. He was steeped in the peace of the heart. Being around him filled you with the same kind of peace and contentment. At the end of his first world tour, Baba told a group of seekers:

> There is no wealth like contentment, no health like contentment, no husband like contentment, and no wife like contentment.[4]

Like courage, contentment is not a passive virtue. In divine contentment, you are not merely pretending to be at peace. In fact, it is a continuous *tapasya*, a wonderful struggle, to "maintain the poise of your heart." Such a beautiful phrase from the poet-saint. But what exactly does it mean: to *struggle* to maintain the poise of the heart?

Why should the heart's well-being take any less effort than the body's well-being? Just as you are attentive to what you feed your body and how you care for it, in the same way you have to be careful what you feed your soul and how you tend to it. It requires steady, quiet effort to keep the heart producing the *rasa*, the sweet flavor, of contentment. You don't just sit back and think, "I don't need anything. Whatever will be will be. *Que será será.*"

Once you taste contentment and start to live in its beauty, you actually want this river of grace to overflow its banks. Living in such contentment gives you the courage to march forward and make the most of this gift of life — life, which is full of difficulties and expectations, full of glory, challenges, promises, purposes, rewards, and failures; life, which is liberating, which lets us create our freedom; life, which is the gateway to enlightenment.

BABA ONCE SAID, "Contentment destroys ego."[5] This is a fascinating statement. It may seem startling to hear that such a benign quality has so much power, that contentment can actually eliminate the most powerful obstacle of all—the ego. Isn't it like hearing that the softest flower petal can blunt the edge of the sharpest sword? Or that one tiny leaf from a rare herb can cure a malignant disease? Or that a slender green vine can cut a huge mountain in two? It may sound farfetched to think that something so small and soft, so delicate and fragile as contentment can obliterate something so big, resistant, and impregnable as the ego.

But then Baba wouldn't say such a thing unless it met four requirements. Baba insisted that spiritual teachings be based on personal experience; backed up by the scriptures; supported by the words of great beings; and finally, blessed by one's own Guru. Therefore, we can be sure that contentment does destroy ego. Contentment is that soft and that powerful. It is truly the most brilliant, life-giving *rasa* there is.

When Baba says, "Contentment destroys ego," this thought-provoking phrase creates a stir in the womb of your knowledge. It begins to breathe new life into your understanding. It animates anything that may have become stagnant or complacent. It makes you move.

Even the slightest bit of contentment has a powerful effect. Haven't you found that the sweet smile of a baby can melt your heart, no matter what you are going through? Wouldn't you be enchanted by the sight of the morning sun reflected in a dewdrop, even if your heart was heavy? Haven't you heard that one sip of water can revive a person who has fainted? Contentment does destroy ego.

What will happen if you let yourself steep in divine contentment and draw your courage from there? It will save you from the enemies of your mind that eat up the serenity of your soul.

Where can contentment truly be found? Contentment arises from knowing that you are with God and God is with you. This experience must be constantly renewed. Then your contentment is always fresh like the dawn and new like the beginning of each year. Again and again, remind yourself, "I am with God, and God is with me. I am with God, and God is with me."

Wake up to your inner courage and become steeped in divine contentment.

RECENTLY I HAD AN AMAZING DREAM. In this dream I was swimming in the ocean with several devotees, as well as some lions and tigers. We were all having a lot of fun. Suddenly, someone shouted to me, "They're coming! They've started!"

We looked up and saw a series of gigantic waves on the horizon. They were still far away, but they were approaching us rapidly. They were huge; they must have towered at least two hundred feet in the air. Everyone else was a terrific swimmer, but I was not. I didn't know how to ride the waves at all. I had no chance of getting away. The waves seemed to gather speed as they approached, and as they came closer, they looked even bigger. I made the decision that the best thing to do was to let go completely and allow myself to slip beneath

the waves as though I were lifeless. I consciously began to surrender to the ocean. I became completely serene, still, and
weightless, so the ocean could wash over me and do anything
it wanted to do with me. From deep within, I knew this was
the most courageous thing I could do— to remain in this state
of tranquility, in this state of meditation, and resist the temptation to struggle.

In that state of total peace, I could still hear the others
crying out, "They're coming! They're coming! The waves are
coming!" All at once, the giant, towering waves started
crashing down upon us. Everyone struggled to stay above
water. Eventually, all of them managed to ride a wave and get
out of there.

I was alone under the tumultuous sea. Yet I did not feel
the least bit helpless. I was in a deep state of tranquility, a
deep state of meditation. My entire being was suffused with
total surrender to the ocean and absolute contentment in this
surrender. It was my choice. I had made a decision to consciously surrender and just be there. After a long time, I
found myself gently washed to the shore, completely unhurt.
My state was unbroken. It was the most profound, blissful
experience of being totally protected. Spontaneously, from
deep inside, these words arose: "I am the daughter of the
ocean. I am the spirit of the ocean."

Everyone was so excited that I was alive. Then we
looked around and saw that one of the lions, who had also
washed up on the shore, was lying there in excruciating pain.
It looked like his back was broken. This lion had thought he
could fight the waves and beat them in a big display of

courage and strength. But now he lay there suffering terribly. He could hardly move. We went and stood by him.

Seeing us, he said, "All of you, learn this lesson from me. I wasn't hurt by the ocean. I was hurt by my own pride."

Whenever you think you are helpless, you are denying God's grace and the Guru's blessings. The minute you turn to the source of grace, the minute you turn to the infinite light of God in your heart, you find the peace and all the protection you need. May you wake up to your inner courage and become steeped in divine contentment.

JANUARY 1, 1997
Shree Muktananda Ashram
South Fallsburg, New York

HOW DOES FEAR, which is such a limiting force, take birth in a living being? The *Viveka Chūdāmani*, a philosophical text by the great eighth-century master, Shankaracharya, says, "Whenever a man, even if he has *viveka*, discrimination, sees the least distinction between himself and the Absolute, the infinite Brahman, fear will arise in him. Such a difference is seen only because of ignorance."[1]

So it is this gap, this apparent difference, that creates fear. As soon as a separation is perceived between the individual soul and the supreme Soul, fear rises in the breach. As long as the union between the individual soul and the Divine is calm and undisturbed, there is total security, absolute joy. There is a sense of sweet blessings and divine splendor embracing everything.

However, as soon as you make a distinction between yourself and the benevolent light, you become fraught with fear. When you think, "I am different from the divine light. The divine light is separate from me. I don't belong to God. God doesn't belong to me. I am different from That"—as soon as there is this chasm, this dislocation, then there is fear. This understanding of the origin of fear has been shared by all the knowers of the Truth, those enlightened souls whose experience of God is constant.

Of course, there is never really any separation between the light and you. Such an idea is an illusion. This is what the scriptures mean by ignorance. It arises from the fact that the senses cannot see the light of God pervading the material world. In their ignorance, the senses misconstrue what they perceive and believe the material world is the only reality. This ignorance is at the root of all fear.

DECEMBER 28, 1996
Shree Muktananda Ashram
South Fallsburg, New York

CHAPTER 2

MEDITATION
and
HAPPINESS

AS YOU DELVE DEEPER INTO THE MESSAGE *Wake up to your inner courage and become steeped in divine contentment,* there are some meaningful questions you might ask yourself: When you are feeling happy, does it occur to you to enter more deeply into your happiness? Do you think about increasing it and prolonging it? Do you ponder what it is made of and where it comes from? Do you inquire into how much more happiness there might be?

One of the great effects of meditation is this: You enter into a deeper relationship with your own happiness, your own contentment. Meditation is all about discovering a vast reservoir of happiness that is yours, ready for you to claim. No matter how happy you think you are, there is so much more happiness inside you just waiting to be experienced. When you explore the inner worlds, what you find is an ocean of contentment.

Meditation is the medium through which you enter into the palace of your heart. Nonetheless, there is a widespread misconception about meditation. People often think you have to be desperate to meditate; you have to be in a state of deep crisis to want to experience God's light. They actually think that when you are feeling completely useless, when you believe you have nothing to offer society, then perhaps it is time to try turning within. Sometimes when people learn that you are meditating, they look at you with a sad face. They think everything must be going very wrong in your life and that's why you need meditation. They think, "What does he have to lose anyway? He might as well meditate." Meditation is ranked at the bottom of the list, the last resort.

My Guru, Baba Muktananda, wrote an extraordinary spiritual autobiography called *Play of Consciousness*. It is a wondrous book. In it, he says, "God exists, but man is in a sad state because he has turned away from Him and lives without faith."[1]

How can you truly describe what God is? God is great, and His greatness is inexhaustible. The more you discover about Him, the more there is to know. God is a mystery, and there will never be a time when you are not baffled by His splendor. To have strong faith in God's existence is in itself a great attainment.

When people talk about God, exactly who and what do they mean? This is a great question and it should be looked into.

The ecstatic Sufi saint Hafiz responds to this question in his poetry. He says:

> I have a thousand brilliant lies
> For the question:
> How are you?
>
> I have a thousand brilliant lies
> For the question:
> What is God?
>
> If you think that the Truth can be known
> From words,
>
> If you think that the Sun and the Ocean
>
> Can pass through that tiny opening
> Called the mouth,

O someone should start laughing!

Someone should start wildly Laughing—
Now! [2]

The saints and sages have their own way of telling us
who God is, what God is. They don't just tell seekers what to
do. Instead, they motivate seekers to look inside and question
aspects of their lives that might otherwise go unnoticed.

ONE DAY A YOUNG STUDENT came to see the great saint
Father Phillip Neri. He told the old man very proudly that he
was going to study law. "I'm really happy," he said. "I have a
good mind, and I'm going to study very hard and become an
excellent lawyer."

"Then what?" asked Father Phillip quietly.

"I'll win all my cases and make a great name for myself."

"And then what?"

"Then I'll be rich. I will build a beautiful house
for myself."

The Father nodded and asked, "And then what?"

"I suppose I'll get married and live to a ripe old age with
the woman I love."

"And then what?"

The student stopped. After some thought, he said,
"Then, like everyone else, one day I'll die."

"And then what?" said the saint.

The young man was disturbed.

Have you ever had an experience like this? When someone says something that brings you very close to your heart,
and you discover something you haven't really wanted to

think about but know you should, you start feeling a little uncomfortable and agitated. You might even get angry at the other person for bringing up an uncomfortable topic that you would rather not discuss.

So the young man was disturbed by the question. Still, he answered gravely, "Then I shall wait for the judgment that will come upon me."

Now the saint said nothing, and the room became still. In this silence, the young man understood something great about himself and the purpose of life.

Such deep silence yields the answer to all questions. Deep silence like this is not passive; it is active. This kind of deep silence is the wellspring of happiness, the source of courage and contentment.

WHERE DOES HAPPINESS LIE? Where do you truly find contentment? If your happiness is anchored in the experience of God, then it is everlasting. You will never come to the end of it. However, if your happiness is based on how smoothly everything is going in your life, how well you are doing, how wonderfully people are praising you, how often you get what you want, how cozy you are in your own little cocoon, then understand that such happiness does not endure. It is illusory by nature. This kind of happiness is something you look for outside yourself. But since change is always taking place, such happiness might not be fully present for you at the moment you need it the most.

Think about it. Is there ever any guarantee that such happiness will be free from hidden desires? Can it stand by itself? Can you be happy merely for the sake of happiness? Or do you need the support of certain circumstances? For example, if your happiness comes from eating a particular type of food, when that food isn't available, then your happiness isn't available either. If your happiness comes from working on a certain project, when you complete the project, then your happiness also disappears. If your happiness comes from succeeding in a certain quest, but that quest is impeded, then you are miserable. If your happiness comes from pleasing certain people, then when they are not pleased for whatever reason, you are left frustrated and anxious. Where is your happiness?

The sages and saints describe this kind of happiness as pleasure, the pleasure of the senses. The senses are happy, but not your heart. This happiness is not deep, and therefore not very stable. It is not true contentment. Haven't you noticed? Many times you give love to someone. You know you are giving love, but they are unable to experience it. In fact, they keep saying you never give them any love. Why can't they experience it? Because the heart isn't happy.

How do you turn toward the light of happiness? First, the scriptures say, accept the possibility—just the possibility —that God dwells within you. You don't have to believe in it; just begin with the possibility. As soon as you do that, you can experience a sweet force moving in your body. That experience is a glimpse of the great light within you.

BABA ONCE SAID, "It is my complete understanding, it is my firm conviction that the human body is the temple of God.

This is not a mere understanding—it has come from my own experience. In this temple, the living God exists. Therefore, I welcome you all with all my heart and with great love."[3]

Baba was a tireless proponent of welcoming. He loved to welcome every person, every animal and plant, every object. On his morning walks, he would look at the trees and say, "Good morning."

I loved to go for walks with him, and when I was little, I thought, "Why does he say 'Good morning' to a tree?"

Later, when Baba was on tour, he would greet the walkers and joggers on his morning walks. And they would all greet him in a friendly way. He extended himself to everything and everyone with all his heart. The moment you saw him, you felt love. It wasn't that you felt *his* love. It wasn't that you felt *your* love. It wasn't that you felt a particular love. You just felt *the* Love, the Love that you want to love. It was tangible and strong. Baba welcomed everyone openly, and he explained why he did this: he looked at a person and saw a temple of God. No matter whom he saw, he saw that person as a temple of God.

Generally speaking, people relate to the human body in one of two ways: either they disregard it as a lump of flesh and bones, or they become obsessed with it. They get quite conceited about it and involve their ego in every move it makes and every outfit it puts on. Where the body is concerned, most people tend to go to extremes, and this does not help create a higher awareness of what the body stands for. Some people fast intensely to overcome the ego's attachment to the body, but for all their efforts, they only become emaciated. They don't even come close to a great inner state. Then there are others who continually pamper their bodies in a million different ways, as if that is where the meaning of life lies.

Now you must definitely think of your basic well-being; you must take care of the body. But we are talking about extremes. Many people ignore the divine light within. They don't understand meditation. They haven't captured the idea of supreme contentment. They haven't yet discovered the divine inner Self, the great light within. Therefore, they choose self-mortification or self-indulgence.

Baba Muktananda said that the human body is a temple of God. He spoke not from abstract understanding or blind faith, but from experience. The ancient *Yajur Veda* is a revealed scripture of India. One of its verses says that this human body you have received is powerful and full of luster. It is meant for meditation and selfless service.[4] It is meant to lead you to God. Your body houses the light of God—what a great awareness to hold on to.

To rediscover this sublime mystery, the ancient sages have given us a wonderful working formula—it is called meditation. Sit quietly for a few minutes now and become aware of your breathing. We will be doing a *dhāranā*, a centering technique that is a great aid to meditation.

For a few moments, think of this divine light that abides in your own being, in your own body. Allow your breath to come in very deep. Allow your breath to go out very long. Think of all the good things you have been able to achieve through your body: the good thoughts you have had, the good words you have spoken, the good actions you have performed. Think of the times you have been joyful and loving in this body. Become aware of how many times you have thought about doing good things for others and how many times you have actually performed those good actions.

Now transcend even the idea of goodness and see what force it is that gives power to goodness. It is the light of your own heart; it is the divine light, which is pure and changeless.

And now breathe naturally.

Your body houses divine light. Your body is the temple of God. The light exists in everything, in all places, and at all times. The more you become conscious of the divine light in your body, the greater you feel about yourself and the greater you feel about the world you live in.

MEDITATION IN SIDDHA YOGA takes place spontaneously through grace. In particular, it takes place through the Guru's grace. It is true that grace is always flowing in everyone's life. No life is devoid of grace. Still, to benefit from its presence, each seeker needs to become a worthy recipient. It is not that grace prefers one person to another, but you have to have the ability to absorb it. Otherwise, it is like pouring water on a hot rock in the desert. As soon as the water hits the rock, it sizzles away before you can blink, even while you are still pouring.

Grace is tremendously powerful, extremely pure, and incredibly sacred. It should never be underestimated and wasted. How can you make yourself receptive to the power of grace? Through meditation. This is why we do centering techniques, so that all your energies come to the region of the heart, the palace of the heart. Then, when you meditate, you are able to experience grace, and meditation happens spontaneously. It is meditation that enables you to hold grace and to let it flourish in your life.

One of the medical doctors who practices Siddha Yoga meditation has told me about the way he takes care of his patients. If you happen to be a student of yoga, he will ask, "Have you been meditating lately?"

Often, the people who go to him will say, "Well, not really."

"Have you been chanting lately?"

"Well, sometimes, but I've been very busy."

"Well, have you been taking some time just to be with yourself, just to be calm?"

"Oh, Doctor, I've been so busy, really so busy. I don't have time for anything."

Then the doctor says, "Listen. My medicine will work better for you when you meditate, when you take some time for yourself. Watch your breathing. Spend some time with yourself. You see, *you* are the best medicine for yourself. And if you can really be with yourself, then you can heal yourself much faster."

Every time I hear about this doctor's advice, it pleases me. He is reminding people that the essence of all healing is to be with themselves. And that is what meditation is.

THE INDIAN SCRIPTURES SPEAK about many stages of meditation. As you continue to meditate, you pass through different layers of deep meditation, or *samādhi.* You reach various states of the mind. This is a vast and subtle subject. However, when you practice meditation through the Guru's grace, you don't need to be concerned about the different levels of meditation. You don't have to wonder, "What layer have I reached?" As long as you remain true to the teachings you receive, as long as you watch and contemplate your inner state, grace will unfold the worlds within you. Grace will guide you, support you, and uplift you every step of the way. When you reach the deepest level of meditation, you enter the sanctum sanctorum of your inner temple. Then all you see is light, the divine light, which is the form of God.

In the *Uddhava Gītā*, Lord Krishna tells his disciple, "With one's mind thus absorbed, one sees Me alone in oneself and sees oneself united with Me, the Self of all—like light merged into light." [5]

What a beautiful image—light merged into light. Knowing God, experiencing God is like light merging into light. Separation ceases to exist, and you experience a wonderful union with your own Self.

Even when you are just beginning, the practice of meditation can be a very accurate gauge of how you are doing in your life. It can tell you something about your inner balance and your relationship with yourself. When you feel good and strong inside, you are able to go into meditation quite easily. On the other hand, when you notice that you have to struggle to get into deep meditation, it may be a sign that you are under some pressure in your life—from your work, your relationships, general anxiety, or fatigue. Meditation helps you to detect how you have been leading your life. Have you been eating excessively? Have you been talking excessively? Have you been thinking excessively?

So don't be discouraged when you experience a certain amount of discomfort in meditation. It is just a passing phase. Meditation actually strengthens you, so that you can look at the parts of your being that you have been afraid to examine.

The other day someone told me he is dreading the start of an exercise regime.

"Why?" I asked.

"Well, when I go to exercise," he said, "I see other people who have progressed so much. They are fit, they are strong, they are enthusiastic. But me, I'm frail, weak. I have no muscles, and they will see how weak I am."

I laughed and said, "They must have gone through that too. They had to begin somewhere, and that is why they are where they are now. You have to begin somewhere, and later on other people will look at you and see how fit and strong and enthusiastic you are."

So you have to begin somewhere. Don't think, "Well, twenty years ago I used to meditate. If I start again now, people will think I'm just a beginner." You know what? It is always great to begin something anew in your life. It is really good. So start your meditation as though it is the first time you have ever meditated. It doesn't matter whether you have ever meditated before. It doesn't matter whether you know how to meditate or not. Just begin. Just let it happen.

Whenever you are afraid to examine yourself, that is a sign you should engage in self-inquiry. When you notice this kind of fear, it actually means you are ready to look within;

you are ready to meditate. If you do this, you go beyond the basic instinct of fear and you show your readiness for transformation. You see, there is readiness within each one of you. Truly, it is there in each moment. All you need to do is learn to ride this wave of readiness, this crest jewel of a wave.

When you learn about yourself, through meditation in particular, you begin to understand that this body is the temple of God and there is a great treasure within. Real glory exists within you, and that is why you go deep into your own being. Meditation uncovers the hidden gems; they are bedazzling and awe-inspiring.

This understanding is at the center of the Indian tradition. As one great being says, "To reach a treasure deeply hidden in the earth, there is nothing to do but dig. In the same way, to have the direct experience of your innermost Self, there is no other means but meditation on the Self."[6]

WE HAVE BEEN EXPLORING the nature of courage and contentment. Ever since the Siddha Yoga tour arrived in Australia, people have been telling me about acts of courage. I was told about the yachtsmen whose boats capsized in the freezing southern ocean. While they exercised great willpower and resourcefulness to stay alive, a truly heroic team of rescuers set out into the stormy seas to save them. The rescuers had the courage and generosity of heart to risk their lives to save these men against extraordinary odds. And there were heartfelt accounts of the courage of the volunteer firefighters during the recent bushfires near Melbourne. These stories are deeply moving.

The message *Wake up to your inner courage*, however, refers to looking deeper into the sustaining power of courage, its inexhaustible nature, its subtleties. This message is about discovering the immense presence of courage, even when no dramatic outer event is calling for courage to arise. Just to sit quietly for a few minutes and plunge deep within your being also takes great courage.

I hear certain complaints over and over, even from people who call themselves advanced meditators. They say, "Every time I sit for meditation, I fall asleep." Or "I stopped meditating because I was afraid I wouldn't be able to function." Or "I can't meditate—there are too many other important things to do." Or they say, "Even if I never actually sit down for meditation, I'm thinking about meditation. That's like meditation, isn't it?" (Baba used to say to people like this, "Well, when you're hungry, why don't you just think about eating?")

Or they say, "My favorite time to meditate is when I'm lying in bed. You know, I turn out the lights and close my eyes. I breathe in deep and breathe out long." Now, they do have a good point here. There is a way to meditate called *shavāsana*, the corpse pose. After you have done hatha yoga postures, you lie flat on your back in a certain position, and you do go into deep meditation.

So some of these points are good; some of these concerns are valid. Nevertheless, if you don't make a genuine effort to understand meditation on its own terms, how far can you really go? If all you do is let your concepts about meditation run around and around, you miss the fruit of meditation.

BABA ALWAYS TALKED ABOUT the tremendous benefits of meditation. He would say, "You should understand that I am a miser."

And we would say, "Really?"

"Yes!" he would repeat. "I am a great miser. You see, I would not have spent my time following the spiritual path, I would not have stayed with my Guru, I would not have meditated if I didn't think all this would bring benefits. Because these things yield wonderful benefits, I spent my time on them, I stuck with them." He would say, "Meditation makes a doctor a better doctor. It makes an engineer a better engineer. It makes a secretary a better secretary. Meditation makes a mother a better mother."

He would say this with such a glow on his face. Not only had he experienced the benefits of meditation for himself, he had seen its blessings in many, many people's lives. For meditation to yield such great benefits, you have to understand what this practice really is.

Why do some people not want to understand meditation? What keeps them away? In the end, it is always some kind of fear.

You would be amazed how many people on the spiritual path are secretly afraid of meditating. But then if you look a little closer, you see that basically they are afraid of everything. Whenever I thought I was afraid of Baba, it was because I had other fears as well. Whenever I thought I was afraid to do something, it wasn't simply one particular thing that scared me, I was afraid of many other things as well. It isn't that people are afraid of meditation only; they are afraid of many other things too, so they constantly manufacture drama in their lives. It's as if all the drama will somehow mask their insecurity; it will hide their fears, and other people won't be able to see what is really going on with them. They may practice this deception knowingly or unknowingly; it doesn't really matter. From whom are they hiding this fear? Most of all, from themselves.

If this description rings a bell for you, take a moment and think about it. You may be afraid of meditation or of the spiritual path. Perhaps you are even afraid of your own innate goodness. If this is the case, isn't it because you are afraid of many other things in your life as well, many people, many projects, and many places? Fear so often holds people back and cuts them off—and not just spiritually.

Where do these fears come from? How are such terrible fears created? Basically, from your own thoughts. You think of something bad, and you are filled with fear. Many of your fearful thoughts are simply habitual, even instinctual. For example, why is a child terrified of being alone in the dark? Why does he invent nightmarish monsters where none exist? Some scientists say it is because mankind's earliest ancestors were constantly under attack by predators. Many thousands of years ago, a child left alone screamed with terror because if his mother didn't come quickly, he would be devoured by a wild beast. Although in modern times babies are raised in a more protected environment, that basic survival response of fear has continued.

There is another way this ancient instinct still operates. Visitors to a baby ward in an orphanage are often surprised by the silence. But consider this: if in early times the mother had abandoned her child, one way for him to hide from wild animals would be to stay very quiet. Some people are afraid to speak up because they feel rejected or abandoned, and they are afraid that those who hear them will attack like predators. So the fear instinct can be expressed either by screaming in terror or by staying completely silent.

The mind conjures up its own fears, makes them a reality, and then suffers because of these fears. If only you would realize that you are much stronger than your fears. Baba once said:

> Thoughts are neither as pure nor as powerful as you are. What can a person who is helplessly robbed by his thoughts hope to achieve in life? Does someone deserve to be called a human being when he allows himself to be plundered by trivial, insignificant, useless, and silly thoughts? Shouldn't a person have self-respect? Shouldn't he be aware of his worth? Shouldn't he have the ability to throw away paltry thoughts and set his mind on the path to God?[7]

WHAT DOES IT MEAN to wake up to your inner courage? It means recognizing your inner purity and the divine power that dwells within you. Anyone who allows himself or herself to be broken down by self-defeating thoughts is actually refusing grace. Understand this: Grace is truly all-embracing. It is not just the Guru's grace that you reject. When you have trouble accepting grace, you also have trouble accepting *anyone's* love. Think of the times when people came forward to help you when you were sick, or perhaps when you were physically unable to move around. But you wanted to do everything for yourself; you couldn't accept their sweetness, their love. They wanted to help you just because they loved you. Why couldn't you experience that love? And even when you did accept love from others, did you fully experience that love?

So it isn't that you refuse only grace: you have a hard time receiving anything valuable. Immediately, you begin to think about how worthless you are, how many terrible things you have done, what a sinner you are. You imagine you will never be able to repay the person. You will never be as good as other people. These self-defeating thoughts make you crumble, and then you live in a dark state. You deprive yourself of the sweet nectar of grace. Truly, it is sweet nectar. Although you long for love, you are not able to accept it and experience it. In this condition, it is no small feat, no small task, to wake up to your inner courage and become steeped in divine contentment.

There is one certain way to accomplish this. In the *Katha Upanishad*, a teacher gives the secret of freedom to a noble seeker. He says: "O Nachiketa, God lives in all bodies; yet He is without a body. He is the eternal and unmoving Reality behind all fleeting and moving things. He is marvelous and all-pervading. Seeing Him in meditation, a person becomes steady, courageous, discerning, and free from sorrow."[8]

Meditation is the way to become aware of your courage. This courage stems from deep within. It is not a fleeting experience like winning a race or performing some outstanding feat. Courage is always with you. Even at quiet times, when nothing in particular is happening, you can feel vast reserves of courage bubbling up within you. You can discover it for yourself. It happens mainly when you realize your own inner purity, when you are in touch with your own Self. Meditation makes this awareness possible. It enables you both to perceive the power within you and to let your inner courage permeate the character of your daily life.

WHEN BABA MUKTANANDA came to the West on his third world tour to impart the Siddha Yoga teachings, he called his mission a "meditation revolution." It was the grace of his Guru that set Baba on the path of meditation and brought him enlightenment. Having attained the ultimate goal, Baba invited everyone to follow in his footsteps, to meditate and become one with God's light. His message was *Meditate on your own Self. Worship your Self. Understand your Self. God dwells within you as you.* What a beautiful golden nugget. Such a profound message. Whenever a great being like Baba extends an invitation, it is a matter of great honor. And to receive that invitation with an open heart is a matter of great good fortune.

We are not talking about meditation as a fad, nor are we talking about dabbling in a few spiritual exercises. We have been given a very strong invitation to meditate from a great Siddha master who can awaken the power of meditation within us. Baba's life and the endless stream of love that flows from him are the greatest support of Siddha Yoga meditation.

THE SUFI SAINT HAFIZ writes about the spiritual path in poems that stun you and wake you up with a start. In one poem he says:

> You have been invited to meet
> The Friend.

No one can resist a Divine Invitation.

That narrows down all our choices
To just two:

We can come to God
Dressed for dancing,

Or

Be carried on a stretcher
To God's ward.[9]

Let's take a minute to think about this. Sit quietly and let your breathing become deep and slow.

You have been invited to meet the Friend. How can anyone resist such a divine invitation? So you have two choices: you can come to God dressed for dancing. Or you can be carried on a stretcher to God's ward.

When and how do you want to reach out to God? How do you want to present yourself? Breathe in deep and breathe out long.

And now breathe naturally.

Entering into a deeper relationship with your own happiness, remember that you have a standing invitation to meditate. You have full permission to enter into a deeper relationship with your own happiness. Be courageous and accept the fact that God dwells within you. Wake up to your inner courage and become steeped in divine contentment.

FEBRUARY 8, 1997
Melbourne, Australia

PLEASE UNDERSTAND, the state of contentment is light-years away from the tendency to become passive or complacent. Its nature is supreme bliss. It comes with the recognition that you are the possessor of a sacred power, the divine *kundalinī shakti*. "Claim this inner power," said Baba Muktananda. "*Kundalinī shakti* belongs to you." It is this conviction that allows you to wake up to your inner courage and savor your own contentment. When you experience deep contentment, you are able to allow this sacred power to shine forth. Suddenly something shifts; your sense of self-worth changes. It moves from a feeling of lack to the most magical feeling of abundance and wholeness. Instead of running here and there in search of love and peace, instead of wasting your time aggravating others by your behavior, you rest in your own fullness.

Contentment comes when you enter into possession of what you already have. An ecstatic feeling
rushes through your entire being. And then wherever
you go, your presence creates a velvety and powerful
effect. It is as if the brilliant moon is walking in.

FEBRUARY 9, 1997
Melbourne, Australia

CHAPTER 3

STEP FORWARD
and
BE THE LIGHT

WAKING UP TO YOUR INNER COURAGE and becoming
steeped in your own inner contentment is one of the sweetest
things you can ever do. When I was in Australia, someone
who came to the programs said to me, "Courage—that I can
accept. But contentment—I don't know about contentment.
I don't know if I want to go so far as to become steeped in
divine contentment. I don't really believe in a spiritual life. I
don't even know if God exists, so I'm not quite sure whether
I want to experience this divine contentment." Then she
paused and said, "Divine contentment! I'm not even sure
about *ordinary* contentment!"

I wish she could have seen herself. She was exuding a wonderful aura of contentment. Just being in her presence, I felt
suffused with contentment. I was admiring her state, her
beauty. She didn't like to talk about spiritual matters, yet she
was tasting and living in the state of contentment.

Sometimes people are afraid to say they experience joy
or they experience the virtues. They like to say, "I don't know
if living a spiritual life is something I can do. I don't know if
I can truly accept it."

This is why we are here—to speak about these things
openly, to explore them openly, to look around and see that
there are many people who are courageous enough to say they
are content, many souls who are daring enough to say they
can experience God. Such people are an inspiration. They fill
you with enthusiasm. They are willing to say contentment is
possible, God is possible.

IN A POETIC REFLECTION addressing seekers, Baba Muktananda once wrote: "Climb on to the bridge of Nityananda. In this way, Muktananda, accomplish your journey with ease."[1]

What does Baba mean—"Climb on to the bridge of Nityananda"? He is telling us to focus on the attributes of his Guru, Bhagawan Nityananda. In a hymn called the *Avadhūta Stotram*, there is a perfect description of Bhagawan Nityananda's state:

> Free of desires, free of expectations, free of defects, independent and fearless—to that Nityananda I bow.
>
> Perfect in yoga, an embodiment of austerity, full of love, having an auspicious countenance, perfect in knowledge, an embodiment of grace—to that Nityananda, I bow.[2]

It is only when you learn how to imbibe the great qualities of a Sadguru, a true master, that you can fully receive what he has to offer. So climbing on to the bridge of Nityananda doesn't mean standing on the back of such a being and reaching for the heavens. It is not as though you step on him and go across to the other shore. Far from it. By meditating on such a being, by concentrating on such a being, by learning from such a being, you rise above the entanglements that keep you bound. You cross over the pitfalls of desires that create anguish. This kind of bridge takes you beyond the expectations that bring about frustration. It lifts you above defects that obscure the goodness of the heart. It breaks the dependency that destroys your self-worth. It annihilates the fear that catapults you into the abyss. This bridge is truly miraculous. By holding fast to the grace of such a being, you are able to find your own divine Self. By experiencing his energy, you truly find yourself in your own heart.

When you attain the company of the Sadguru, of a great being like Bhagawan Nityananda, then instead of struggling with the whirlpool of desires, the raging fire of expectations, the deluge of defects, the quicksand of dependency, and the hurricane of fears, you are guided and supported by benevolent light. You drink the wisdom of the Siddhas instead of the poison of others' negativities. You behold this light and keep moving forward until finally you merge into it. In this way, you are not crippled by obstacles and limitations. You are liberated by God's light. This freedom feels so much better than sinking your teeth into a mass of poisonous qualities. By meditating on the auspicious countenance of such a being, you begin to recognize the auspiciousness within yourself.

Why do so many people love to go to the Bhagawan Nityananda Temple and behold his auspicious countenance? When we perceive him, it is not just in him we see the glorious face—it is in our own hearts. We feel warm liquid honey permeating our being. We appear before him because of what he makes us feel inside. Over and over again, we come for his darshan —his auspicious countenance, his face, his hands, his feet, his entire being. Everything about him is auspicious. And you feel *mangala*, auspiciousness, inside; you feel your own greatness. Then whatever you see is a good omen, a blessed omen. You yourself become a good omen. When people see you, they want to come and speak to you. When others are in your presence, they know something great will happen. The supreme light is reflected clearly in you, and it fills the world around you.

When you behold the face of Bhagawan Nityananda, you take the light with you. Then it is possible to live Baba Muktananda's potent message: "See God in each other." You are able to recognize that God lives in everyone, God is everyone's friend, God belongs to all.

TUKADYADAS WAS A GREAT POET-SAINT. He was also one of Baba Muktananda's Siddha friends. In one of his songs, he says:

O Lord, You exist in every country,
 in every form and appearance.
Your names are countless, but You are essentially one.
This world is a stage for Your divine play.
You pervade every action and emotion
 on this divine stage.

When you practice seeing the Lord in your own heart and in everyone else, you make these words of Tukadyadas come true. You let God shine forth. You truly become God's friend. You don't have to proclaim to the world, "I am God's friend." Just seeing you, people know it is true. You manifest the immensity of God's splendor.

Baba Muktananda once said, "The Siddha Yoga meditation revolution is based on high principles. The highest principle is the Self; it is light, it is love, and it is peace. Through the Self, we experience that same love toward everyone." [3]

When you embrace and practice this great teaching, you experience supreme love for all of God's creatures. You show your deep yearning to know God, and at the same time, you respect God's light in all sentient beings and insentient objects. This is the supreme quest.

"The highest principle is the Self," said Baba. "It is light, it is love, and it is peace." Just remembering these words of Baba and translating them into your daily activities will give you everything you are looking for.

Each time you find it difficult to interact with someone, think of what Baba said about the highest principle: it is light, it is love, and it is peace. At such moments, allow your own pure wisdom to shine forth. Instead of waiting for the other person to shower you with light, you step forward and be the light. Instead of waiting for the other person to reveal love, you step forward and be the embodiment of love. Instead of waiting for the other person to come to terms with his or her anger, you step forward and be the messenger of peace, the highest principle. Remember, Bade Baba is a being of auspicious countenance, a glorious being. Allow your auspiciousness to permeate your world. In this way, you wake up to your own inner courage and become steeped in divine contentment.

Being courageous doesn't mean carrying a gleaming sword and telling everyone else to be quiet. Divine contentment doesn't mean you lie down on a grassy hill and let everyone else do the work. You need courage to see the inner light.

In the *Bhagavad Gītā*, Arjuna begs Lord Krishna to show him his divine, true form. The Lord warns him he isn't ready for it. But Arjuna won't listen; he wants it right away. The Lord obliges. Instantly, millions of suns burst forth. The light is incredible and Arjuna is terrified; he can't tolerate the brilliance of this splendor. You do need courage to experience the divine light.

To become steeped in divine contentment is not just putting your head on the pillow and thinking, "I feel content today." It is not eating an ice cream cone and saying, "Now I'm experiencing true contentment in my being." No, it is something very different. When the experience of deep contentment takes place, you don't even exist to talk about it. This is why it is difficult to speak about the virtues, about the attributes of God. Once you experience them, you melt. Light merges into light. Love merges into love. Peace merges into peace.

WAKE UP TO YOUR INNER COURAGE and experience the ease of the heart. You can do this if you truly imbibe the words of Tukadyadas:

> O Lord, You are the one who rises from the ocean
>   and forms clouds.
> You are the clouds that burst
>   and the rain that pours down.
> You then flow as streams and mighty rivers.
> In all these varying forms, O Lord, it is just You.
> It is You alone who exist.
>
> O Lord, You are in every country, in every costume.
> You are in every language.
> You delight in every heart.
>
> O Lord, You exist in every country
>   in every form and appearance.
> Your names are countless, but You are essentially one.
>
> You manifest as a tiny ant,
>   and You are the one who pervades this universe
>   as particles and atoms.
> You become every form of life.

In some places, You are great mountains.
In other places, You stand in the form of huge trees.
All the beauty that can be seen in this universe
    is a reflection of You, O Lord.
You and this beauty are truly one.

Truly, this is the highest understanding one can have. Nonetheless, you must have great fortune to see the world with these clear eyes. You have to have clear and strong eyes to see God as God. You need the grace of the Sadguru.

As Tukadyadas says:

O Lord, You exist in every country,
    in every form and appearance.
Your names are countless, but You are essentially one.
My Sadguru has given me this divine vision
    through his grace.
I am able to chant the Lord's name
    day in and day out.
Tukadyadas says:
By holding His name in my heart,
    all the distinctions of mine and yours
    and all sense of duality merge into oneness.
My Sadguru has bestowed divine vision upon me.

TO RECOGNIZE AND LIVE this great truth, to comprehend the experiences you are having, it is essential to study the scriptures and understand them in depth. With knowledge of the scriptures, you will come to understand what you have received. Your tongue will refuse to speak badly of God's universe. Your ears will not seek to hear horrible things. The goddess Saraswati will play on your tongue. She is beautiful. She will dance; she will play her *vīnā*. Your heart will be permeated with the knowledge of the all-pervasive Truth. In each face, you will be able to see the light of God. In each difficulty, you will see the Blue Pearl shining. Your vision will change completely. As you study the scriptures, your experience of the great shakti will become more concrete. You will understand it in a very different way.

People who truly know and experience the scriptures understand things not just from books but from the heart. And the heart is the greatest library. It stores all the wonderful experiences you have had in your sadhana. Scholars who are doing spiritual practices don't merely examine topics; they actually dive into the content. They don't have to be outside of their practices to speak objectively about their path. They can be practicing, learning, and teaching at the same time. They have a broader context for everything, so even if they hear something negative, they are able to see it from a different viewpoint. When you study the scriptures, your vision changes.

Some people have been on the spiritual path for a long time, and somehow, even though they have received shaktipat, their tongue hasn't changed its color; it still has a poisonous coating. Although their hearts have been transformed by initiation, by grace, their tongues do not reveal that. Their tongues still spew forth poisonous venom. Their eyes still have cataracts. And therefore, they still cannot see God's love permeating this universe.

People who study and experience the scriptures can help others to understand the teachings. They can teach the scriptures in such a way that you understand what your experience is about. Everyone who has received shaktipat and who does spiritual practices eventually has deep, classical experiences. But unless you have a scriptural context, you don't really understand their worth. Many, many of you are carrying treasures, jewels of wisdom. But because you don't know how the scriptures describe and explain these matters, you think, "Oh, I've just received this little thing. I haven't gotten enough." You feel a lack of contentment. Once you have studied the scriptures and seen what you really have, waking up to your inner courage will bear fruit for you. You will experience deep contentment.

When you study the scriptures, don't worry too much about whether you understand everything right away. Just read them. Even just reading will do a lot of good. As you understand something, write it down. And if you read something that you already know, don't pass over it, saying, "I already know this." Understand it from another angle.

When you imbibe the scriptures, the poisonous coating on your tongue will be cleansed, the cataracts from your eyes will be removed, the wax from your ears will be dissolved, your nostrils will be purified, your throat will be cleared. Then the light of the heart can shine forth. You will truly understand the worth of shaktipat and the grace that you receive from the Guru. You will come to realize what it is to have a living master in your life, what it is to have the grace of the Siddhas protecting you each moment. And then you will be able to understand Tukadyadas' words even more deeply:

O Lord, You exist in every country, in every costume.
This world is the divine stage
    for Your play of Consciousness.

TAKE A MOMENT NOW and recollect what Baba Muktananda said: "The highest principle is light, it is love, and it is peace." Contemplate your own pure wisdom shining forth. Instead of waiting for another person to shower you with light, you step forward and be the light. Instead of waiting for someone else to reveal love, you step forward as the embodiment of love. Instead of waiting for the other person to come to terms with his anger, you step forward and be the messenger of peace.

Allow your own auspiciousness to permeate the world you live in. Meditate on the auspiciousness that spreads within you and around you. Allow the light of auspiciousness to pierce through all the layers of your body. Allow this light to pierce through all the layers of the mind. Allow it to pierce your speech. Allow the auspiciousness in your heart to rise up and fill your entire being with love. Allow this love to multiply itself a thousandfold so that you become a messenger of peace.

As you go about your daily activities, see if you can let greater goodness and beauty and auspiciousness come forth. Learn to experience gratitude for everything you are given, so that what you are receiving in so many forms will continue to grow. In that way, you will be able to receive more and more. Let your gratitude grow, so that you can stay connected to the vessel of nectar within. You want to keep the vessel of nectar strong and shining. Understand that everything you receive is a gift, that you are very fortunate. Even to put your feet on the spiritual path, to enter the Temple, to behold the auspicious countenance of a great being—all this is due to your good fortune and to the great hearts of those who offer so much service to this path.

AUGUST 2, 1997
Shree Muktananda Ashram
South Fallsburg, New York

THERE IS SOMETHING I want to make very clear: the experience of divine love makes you extremely strong. The experience of the Truth, of supreme Consciousness, does not make you feeble. It does not weaken you. Sometimes people have the understanding that if you are immersed in God's love, you should wear a syrupy smile and always say Yes to everything; you should never contradict anyone. Baba used to say that many people would like to have a spineless Guru. But weakness is not what he taught, and it is not what he lived.

The experience of love has great strength; the experience of divinity is very powerful. This does not mean you have to behave in a particular way. You let your strength and courage come forward naturally. When it is time to say No, you say No with courage and dignity. When it is time to say Yes, you say Yes with the same courage and dignity.

Please understand that being inside out is your strength. It doesn't mean you are so vulnerable that you can no longer function in this world. Being inside out, your strength shimmers in the air.

AUGUST 29, 1997
Shree Muktananda Ashram
South Fallsburg, New York

CHAPTER 4

THE COURAGE
to
KNOW
your own
WORTHINESS

YESTERDAY EVENING I RECEIVED a very sweet message from someone asking me to look outside my window. I did—and there was a gorgeous rainbow. It was the first time I had been able to see the lavender color so distinctly. It was pristine. The rainbow was also incredibly wide, and against the dark Krishna clouds, it shone forth wonderfully. It felt like a gift.

The Indian tradition says that at midnight on this day, Krishna was born, and it is believed that he will be born over and over again. In the *Bhagavad Gītā*, Lord Krishna promises: "I will take birth in this world again and again."[1] He says: "Whenever there is the fall of righteousness, whenever the saints are persecuted, I will take birth to show the world a true way."[2] Nonetheless, it has been my experience that the Lord takes birth when there is righteousness as well. When you experience righteousness in your heart, that is the birth of the Lord. Whenever you experience inner light, the Lord is present. So God takes birth within our being again and again. This is why every moment is fresh, every moment is full of energy.

IT IS WONDERFUL THAT so many of you have collected your courage and are seeking to know your own worthiness. It is such a delicate matter—worthiness. As much as you want love, you doubt if you are worthy to receive it. As much as you want knowledge, you wonder, "Am I really worthy enough to have knowledge?" As much as you want great friends in your life, you doubt what will happen once they truly know who you are. There is always doubt about your worthiness. The doubt isn't so much, "Will that person give me love? Will he give me knowledge? Will she be my true friend?" Those doubts somehow do get removed sooner or later. It's the doubt about innate worthiness that plagues everyone. Not just now and then, but much of the time, it drags a person down. This is why I say you are courageous in seeking to know your own worthiness. You never know what you are going to find out in the process.

You are pursuing a great endeavor. You don't have to be too concerned about the end result. If you think only about the end result, then you may break down in the middle. If you have the courage to move on, the stamina to continue, that is what will bear the greatest fruit. So don't focus on the end result. You will never know your own worthiness in that way. You must move on from wherever you are. And you needn't wonder whether you are at the beginning or the middle or close to your destination. Wherever you are, that is the perfect place for you to be. It may be comfortable or uncomfortable; it may be happy or very sad. It really doesn't matter. Your whole journey is to go deeper into your own Self, higher into your own Self. All the rough edges that confront you won't hold you back. If you persevere, they will actually help you to go further, to travel deeper into the ocean of knowledge, the ocean of love. And that is exactly what we do on this path. We plunge into the ocean of the great Self; we dive into the ocean of love. And how do we do this? We meditate.

MEDITATION IS A MYSTICAL PROCESS. Although in this modern age meditation is sometimes used as a tool to reduce blood pressure and anxiety and to bring about good health in general, still it is a mystical process. Meditation is a mystical alchemy. What happens in meditation is beyond the reach of the senses. The fringe benefits may be that high blood pressure goes down, pain is relieved, anxiety becomes less. But these are just fringe benefits. What truly happens is golden; it has the luster of thousands of diamonds. It brings about deep tranquility. Once you experience this gift of meditation, you will never want to trade it for anything else. In fact, it becomes your compass, your gauge. You always know where to go to find deep tranquility. This is God. This is supreme love. This is the highest knowledge.

Many of you may doubt whether you really go into meditation. This kind of doubt is beneficial. It makes you want to learn more about your Self; it makes you eager for deeper meditation. If you knew you could get into meditation in a flash, just imagine how big your ego would become. Many people do say they can go into meditation just like that! But when you see their faces, you want to run away. Then there are others who say, "No matter how much I try, I can't get into meditation. I don't think I really go into meditation." And with these people you feel a bond because they are in touch with themselves. They *are* going into meditation. It's just that they don't want to stop where they are; they want to look deeper. They are the true scientists on the spiritual path. Their yearning is so great that they want to keep meditating. They are not satisfied with just getting into meditation; they want to explore further. They want to be in that state all the time. So the doubt you have about whether you go into meditation or not is a beneficial doubt, a healthy doubt.

On the one hand, you keep trying; on the other hand, grace makes it happen. Grace and your effort come together, and you have a beautiful process in hand. Always remember: Grace wants to be with you. It is up to you how you approach grace.

We all have different personalities. Some people are flamboyant. They make a dramatic expression of knowing this person and that person, of knowing the Guru. They are demonstrative about everything. Then there are other personalities, quiet and indrawn, minding their own business. Other types often get angry and ask, "Why is it like this? Why don't people pay more attention to me?" Other people are gentle and poetic: "Oh, look, the flower is blooming; it's so fragrant." And so it goes, from one personality to another.

In the same way, there are many approaches to meditation and many ways meditation approaches you. Some meditations are deep and quiet. Some meditations are loud and full of physical movements. Others are full of wisdom, with one revelation after another, one intuition after another. It is almost as though the cosmic book opens before you. You have answers to everything, and you are mesmerized by what you are hearing, what you are seeing in your meditation. Some people hear divine sounds in meditation, and they are totally enchanted by what they hear. Whatever happens in your meditation, that is what should happen.

Sometimes people feel completely numb. I remember experiencing a numb state in meditation that would continue into my daily activities. Once I asked Baba if I should stop meditating because every time I meditated, I became numb. I had no feeling, no thought, no desire. I didn't even want to live. There was no desire to do anything, to be anything. But Baba said, "No, that's a very good state. It's what happens at a certain stage in meditation. You should accept it." And when I accepted that state, I began to relish it.

So different states emerge in meditation. Sometimes you may be sitting in meditation, and you can hear your mind going *Chomp! chomp! chomp!* And you get so frustrated! You think, "When will my mind stop chomping? Chomping down on this thought! Chomping down on that thought! Not digesting anything, but just *chomp! chomp! chomp!*" Sometimes it seems as if the mind is cutting down trees. You might feel that it will drive you crazy. You might even think you need to take some medication.

At such times, the best thing to do is to repeat the mantra *Om Namah Shivāya*, which means "I honor the Lord, who dwells in my heart." Just *Om Namah Shivāya*. Truly, it does work. *Om Namah Shivāya* takes you to an incredible state. Even if it's just for a few minutes, you do go to an entirely different place. So if this kind of chomping takes place during meditation, just repeat the mantra mentally, "*Om Namah Shivāya, Om Namah Shivāya.*" In a way, this experience of chomping is good because your mind becomes so exhausted that finally it gives in and says, "Oh, please! I'll take *Om Namah Shivāya.*"

Anything that happens during meditation will be a great lesson. It will release an incredible alchemy within you. Intellectually, you may not always be able to understand it, and that is fine. Just allow yourself to fall into the state of meditation.

Grace always seeks you; it always wants you. No matter how often you may think you are not worthy, grace always finds you worthy. Blessings are plentiful. Just allow yourself to glide into meditation. No matter how many obstacles there seem to be, don't worry about them; don't worry about anything.

To go into meditation, you have to go beyond the layers of discomfort, anxiety, and panic. You call on your inner courage as much as possible and just allow yourself to relax, to settle into your own shakti, to have trust. Within you is a mystical world. If you just go into it naturally, it will reveal itself to you. If you try too hard to open the door to this mystical world, you will only end up with your own effort. Very gently, very comfortably, if you follow the path of the breath, if you let yourself glide into meditation, then you will really soar.

NO MATTER HOW MUCH LOVE YOU RECEIVE, there is always more that will come your way. No matter how much worthiness you experience, there is still more to experience. This is the mystery of love, the mystery of worthiness. There is plenitude in God's world.

Baba Muktananda's great teaching is "Meditate on your own Self, worship your own Self, understand your own Self, kneel to your own Self, honor your own Self. God dwells within you as you." When you have this experience, then you know your own worthiness.

The human heart is a blessed gift from God. It is sacred; it houses the divine light. The entire body is a sacred present from God. This very body contains infinite mystical experiences, boundless compassion, steady benevolence, tremendous patience, tender kindness, innate goodness, pure innocence, and loving strength. As you realize more fully the divine light embodied in your heart, you recognize it outside yourself as well—in a person, in an object, in a moment, in a place.

Every time you accept your own worthiness, you are creating a paradise—not just where you are, but also in other places in the world. Every time you experience your own love, you are supporting thousands of lives.

Allow yourself to honor the God within. Allow yourself to know your own true worthiness. And may you have greater understanding of everything that will unfold in your life. It is such a blessed gift from God to realize that you deserve love: you deserve to give love and you deserve to be loved.

Thank you for taking the teachings you have digested wherever you go, for taking them to the rest of the world. Your love is going to nourish the world. Thank you very much. I love you.

AUGUST 23, 1997
Shree Muktananda Ashram
South Fallsburg, New York

TRUE COURAGE is interwoven with humility. Like courage, humility contains immense power. Being humble does not mean being weak or meek. Real humility arises naturally when you recognize the great light, the divine power that exists, not only within you but within all equally. Humble people may appear very mild, but in reality they have great strength. In the same way, courageous people may seem bold and self-sufficient, but in reality their hearts are filled with humility because they know their courage flows from a divine force. Humility and courage are interwoven.

It doesn't matter what life sets before you—good advice, a student loan, food, the bounty of nature, or a gentle admonishment—receive it with a humble heart. Whatever comes your way—added responsibility, a heartfelt compliment, a promotion, a windfall, unexpected suffering, an unpleasant neighbor, or people who make your life difficult—humility is always the noblest response. It is also the most constructive.

If you are humble, then, in a most natural way, these situations will either expand or diminish, depending on what needs to happen at any given moment. Good things will endure and misfortune will dwindle. With humility, you are able to benefit from good fortune and become free from sorrow. Therefore, follow in the footsteps of the courageous ones. Follow the path of courage.

FEBRUARY 9, 1997
Melbourne, Australia

CHAPTER 5

THE STEADINESS

of

GOD'S PRESENCE

THIS IS AN AUSPICIOUS GATHERING here in the California desert. I love the desert. It holds great magical power. It wraps you in its stark and mysterious blanket and prepares you to enter a mystical world. Today is the auspicious day of the full moon, the moon that sheds benevolent rays so brightly in the clear desert sky. I was told that the Hopi Indians call this particular full moon the Hawk Moon. They also say it is the Initiate's Moon—perfect for shaktipat.

The message we have been exploring for some time now is *Wake up to your inner courage and become steeped in divine contentment.* One of the ancient hymns of the *Atharva Veda* says:

> May we be without fear
> of friend and foe.
> May we be without fear
> of the known and the unknown.
> May we be without fear
> by day and by night.
> Let all the world be my friend.[1]

What a sweet and courageous invocation! It rings with the power of courage, the power to overcome the many faces of fear. Becoming free of fear is so important to a seeker. Not until the final masks of fear vanish can you be truly free. Fear keeps you in bondage; courage makes you experience your own freedom. Fear keeps you from embracing the highest love. Fear keeps you from delighting in nature's bounty. Fear keeps you from reveling in the beauty of God. Fear keeps you from respecting another person's religion. It keeps you from accepting another person's love for God. Fear keeps you from giving blessings to the faith of others. Fear keeps you from loving your community. Fear keeps you from loving the love in your own heart.

This prayer in the *Atharva Veda* asks the Lord to banish fear and kindle the light within. It invokes the courage to embrace the inner light. The message of this hymn is uplifting: it urges you to rise above fear, to shed all impurities, to reach for the light in your own heart. And as you offer this prayer, you ask for the strength to perceive the whole world as your friend. Of course, this is an enormous undertaking. You need great courage to allow this generous friendship to take place. You must let go of pettiness and impurities. Then you will notice goodness shimmering in your heart, goodness suffusing your entire life with its splendor.

I LOVE TO WATCH the first light of the sun as it strikes the peak of a mountain. It is gorgeous. As the sun begins to rise, the mountain that has lain very still through the night receives a golden crown. Within a few seconds, the sun seems to drape the mountain in the light of its own being. It is marvelous to see how the different elements of nature embrace one another in the light of the sun right before your eyes.

Spiritual practices are like the rising of the sun. Meditation, chanting, contemplation, selfless service, repetition of the mantra—these practices bring freshness and radiance to everything they touch. When the first light of the morning sun hits the mountains, they look pink and red and golden. As time goes by, they become platinum, covered with the white light of the sun. As you allow yourself to go deeper into the practices, you will notice the same thing happening within your own being.

After a person has been doing spiritual practices for a concentrated period of time, others often ask, "What's happened to you? You look so radiant! Are you in love?" When your heart is awakened, your entire being is lit up with its beauty, its courage. As you give yourself to the wonderful, timeless practices, they burn away the pollution that has collected in your life. They dispel the clouds that obscure your own sense of worth. They bring forth the gladness of the heart. And truly, your heart is always glad—so let yourself experience it!

Baba Muktananda often spoke of the need to accept the divinity shining within the human heart. Once he said: "Man is not the inadequate creature he may appear. He is sublime and only harms himself because he is unaware of his own worth."[2]

Baba's words are simple yet profound. They awaken you to the glory of your own heart. Hearing them, you realize there is a greater you that is full of God's light. As Baba said: "You are sublime; you are worthy. Why do you suffer?" You suffer because you think you are not good enough. When do you experience divinity? It is when you know: *I am sublime; I am worthy.* This is when you experience true gladness of heart.

Therefore, instead of sinking into a morass of fear and failure, soar with the wisdom of the heart. Then you will find yourself climbing the true ladder to success. With each step, you become lighter and more buoyant. These words *sublime* and *worthy* can have an extraordinary impact on your life. They summon you to enter the realm beyond fear.

LET'S PAUSE FOR A FEW MOMENTS NOW and contemplate Baba's words. We will do a short *dhāranā*, a centering technique in which you hold the mind steady on a single thought of a divine nature. When you quiet the mind by focusing on something divine, such as the words of a great being, you touch the natural state of the Self.

As the breath gently flows in and out, take Baba's words into your heart: *I am sublime; I am worthy.* These words carry you to the place inside that is full of God's light, a place beyond all fear and failure where your inner glory is always blazing.

I am sublime; I am worthy. This place can never be touched by the ups and downs of life. No matter what is going on in your life, know that you are sublime, you are worthy. You can find this place in a moment. Simply hold the radiant thought: *I am sublime; I am worthy.*

As the breath comes in, *I am sublime.* As the breath goes out, *I am worthy.* Breathe in, *I am sublime.* Breathe out, *I am worthy.*

And now breathe naturally.

Let the power of Baba's words carry you beyond all fear into the wisdom of the heart. To contemplate *I am sublime; I am worthy* is to wake up to your inner courage and become steeped in divine contentment.

It is an exhilarating practice to experience the radiant wisdom in the words of great beings. Baba Muktananda experienced the worthiness, the sublimity of the heart, and because of this attainment, he could give the same experience to others.

RECOGNIZING YOUR OWN INNER SELF, knowing the truth of the words "I am sublime; I am worthy," is not egotistical. You are not saying, "I am sublime; I am better than others. I am worthy; I am better than others." No. You are recognizing the glory in your own heart that also exists in everyone else's heart. This recognition allows you to wake up to your inner courage and become steeped in divine contentment. Truly, when you touch your heart, you touch God.

We have been talking about courage, about being at ease and experiencing your own contentment. How do you extract the essence of this message? How do you keep the experience constant? In a *bhajan*, a devotional song, the nineteenth-century poet Padmakar describes how you can speak to the Lord in your own heart, and how you can keep your understanding sublime at all times:

O my courageous heart, have patience.
If you can hold on bravely for some time,
    you will see that the bad times
    will take a turn for the better.
Just as sorrow came after happiness,
    in the same way, after some time
    happiness too will follow sorrow.
O my courageous heart, have patience.
Just as we constantly listen
    to the sweet music of Krishna's flute,
    so will Krishna hear us calling out His name
    and come be with us.
Some day, sooner or later, the good days do return.

"O my courageous heart, have patience." How do you cultivate this patience? The knowers of the Truth, of pure being, give this advice: Focus on the steadiness of God's presence. Think about the steady power of the Siddhas in your life. Contemplate their constant love. If you can just focus on this awareness, you experience your own goodness all the time, and then you have patience. Whatever you do, you will do with graceful movement. You won't be in a hurry. And even if you are in a hurry, you will take the time to wonder at God's beauty.

This morning as I was coming to the program, I thought I wasn't keeping very good time, so I was hurrying a bit. Then I saw a beautiful golden butterfly flying back and forth right in front of me. I was moving quickly, but something said, "Stop! You have time to look at the butterfly and thank God for his beauty." And the butterfly began to dance. This was the first time I had ever seen a butterfly dancing for so long in one place. Usually they are fickle, but today this butterfly had such patience. As he danced and danced, he was teaching me about patience.

I kept looking at the butterfly, and as I watched, I realized I had all the time in the world. I became very, very still. Even now, I can see that delightful butterfly dancing before me. When I came into the hall today and saw all of you, I thought, "Ah! There are hundreds of butterflies here!" Even though your hearts are dancing, there is such stillness in the air.

Focus on the steadiness of God's presence in your life. When you feel bad, when you are in a hurry, when you are down in the dumps, when you think you cannot take another step, focus your attention on the steadiness of God's presence. When you are elated, when you are excited, when you are enthusiastic, when you are soaring, focus your attention on the steadiness of God's presence. Just as the divine *mūrti*, the statue, of Bhagawan Nityananda is always steady in the Temple, in the same way, the presence of God is always manifest in your heart. So take a little extra time to behold a waterfall, to marvel at the snow on a mountain peak. And then, when you sit down to realize your own sublimity, your own worthiness, take time and focus on the steadiness of God's presence. This practice will definitely teach you patience; it will give you the gold mine of patience.

When you focus on the steadiness of God's presence within, your heart is filled with courage. This courage of the heart allows you to get through times of sorrow with great patience. Although such times may seem difficult and barren, if you are watchful, you are able to unearth miraculous gems, priceless jewels. Do not flee from such moments, no matter how uncomfortable you may feel. It is during your most difficult moments that you have the greatest experience of God. Whatever the discomfort, learn to go through it. If you make a mistake, don't try to ignore it and run away. Stay with it; rise above it. When you try to avoid the times of sorrow, your time is spent in anger and frustration. You continually mull over your helplessness. You keep bringing your miseries to the forefront of your mind. Your emotions are colored with painful memories. In this way, you thoroughly dampen your spirits. And then your suffering weighs so much that your heart refuses to rise to the occasion.

How does a seeker keep the heart strong in the throes of adversity? Where can you turn for sustaining support? Focus on the steadiness of God's presence in your heart, in your life. Whatever you think about, that is what you become.

WHEN A SMALL CHILD IS HELD close to his mother's bosom, he feels totally protected. Whether the mother is walking through a crowded lane, a threatening forest, or a dark tunnel, the child remains quite content and happy. The warmth of the mother's heart keeps the child feeling secure and much loved. Similarly, when your attention is fastened on God's presence, on divine grace, you are able to maintain a state of equipoise, of comfort. With such steadfastness, you inherit divine contentment and shine with God's radiance. You are able to welcome difficulties with a courageous heart.

You have a choice: you can go through life whining and complaining, or you can live your life with dignity and sublime poise. If you think the more you whine, the more attention you will get, you are mistaken. In the moment people may come forward to help you. They may like it when they see an underdog; their hearts may bleed. But remember, they will not have much respect for you. They will talk about you to others: "Oh, that person—he cries at the drop of a hat." "Oh, that person—you can't really talk to her. She's always complaining and blaming others."

At the time, you think they are helping. And they *are* helping; it is the nature of the human heart to help when someone is suffering or in distress. But you will not receive the respect worthy of an individual who has God dwelling inside. People will sympathize with you; they will have empathy; they will console you. But you can gain their respect only by sharing the goodness of your heart, the courage of your heart. Then they will remember you. They will say, "That person—I want to be with her. She makes me feel my own courage and strength." "That person makes me feel happy with myself."

Now that is how you should be remembered. That is true respect. When you hold the steadiness of God's presence in your heart, the steadiness of divine grace, you feel secure; you feel very much loved. Grace is the uplifting force in your life.

BABA'S WORDS ARE BEACONS along the spiritual path. He says:

> If the mind is full of doubts, it affects your ability
> to make a right decision. Your heart should be full of
> courage. It is on account of fear that you keep wavering
> between alternatives. And on account of that wavering,
> you make the wrong decision. Through meditation, if
> you could get within the reach of the inner Self, then
> your decisions would be quite dependable. Your heart
> should be full of courage. Meditate intensely; the inner
> Self always makes the right decision.[3]

Baba always stresses the wonder of meditation. Meditation strengthens every cell of your heart. Meditation regenerates hopefulness. Meditation radiates tendrils of faith and makes them grow very strong. Through meditation, you reach the inner Self. Then when you make a decision, it springs from an unwavering state of consciousness. It is not influenced by worldly matters that ebb and flow. Rather, it originates from the deep inspiration of the inner Self. Such a decision is unshakable. You can rely completely on its validity. You can rest your whole life on it.

I love the way Baba says so straightforwardly, "Your heart should be full of courage." For a moment, let us step into the certainty of his words as we do a brief *dhāranā*, a centering exercise.

Allow the mind to focus on the breath as it flows in and out. Allow the mind and body to relax. With every inbreath and every outbreath, feel your heart expanding.

And now, repeat to yourself: *My heart is full of courage. My heart is full of courage.* Within you is a wellspring of courage. You know its waters very well. You dip into them each time life asks you to step beyond what is easy, what is familiar, what is convenient. You drink from the source quite often. *My heart is full of courage.*

Reach into the clear water of courage and take a drink. How pure it is. How invigorating the taste. When you really think about it, your courageous heart has carried you through many ordeals. It has uplifted you through countless challenges. It has helped you to take leaps that have changed your life completely. Let your breathing continue to be deep and full.

Hold this truth within your own being: *My heart is full of courage. My heart is full of courage.* Treasure the inspiration of the courageous heart and draw strength from its never-ending presence. It exists within each and every one of you. Always remember: *My heart is full of courage.*

And now breathe naturally.

Baba's words fill a seeker with strength. They can make you feel there is so much within you that is great. They can make you feel that you are worth more than a gold mine, that you are ready for the goal.

As you give yourself to spiritual practices, you wake up to your own inner courage, and very naturally that courage bears the sweetest fruit of divine contentment. Contentment enables you to rest in the arms of God's unending love. You revel in the knowledge that life is a gift you are continually opening. You think you have experienced love, but then there is more, there is more. You think your heart cannot stretch any further, it has reached its limit, but then it expands even more. New vistas appear before you, and their landscapes are touched by the sunlight of awakened understanding. You are always rediscovering the magic of life.

Take these moments to marvel at the magic of your heart. Take these moments to send your blessings and good wishes to the people you know. Take these moments to offer your gratitude to the Almighty.

Remember, when you feel wonderful, when you feel sorrowful, God is there. Rest in this awareness. Focus on the steadiness of God's presence in your heart. Recognize this divine presence in your life.

DECEMBER 13, 1997
Palm Springs, California

TO GAIN ACCESS to your own courage, you must develop the ability to observe discipline. Discipline helps you to cultivate the constant awareness of your energy as divine, as something to be gathered, protected, and preserved. Steady discipline allows you to collect the great wisdom of the Siddhas. It allows you to store the precious jewel-like virtues. Steady discipline allows you to safeguard the fruits of your sadhana. It allows you to preserve faith and devotion. Steady discipline allows you to watch over the fire of awakened energy, *kundalinī shakti*. Steady discipline truly is a boon from the Guru, a boon from the fortune of your many lifetimes. Steady discipline comes from grace. It is grace that allows you to follow discipline.

Once you become anchored in steady discipline, you will breathe freely. You will breathe ecstatically. You will feel you are walking on a magic carpet. Your whole life will be filled with miracles of transformation. Your life itself will be a miracle of transformation. You will experience, "My life is blessed. My life is blessed. My life is blessed." You will be steeped in divine contentment. You will experience courage and contentment wherever you go—in your office, in your kitchen, when you play with your children, when you talk to your friends, and when you observe silence. You won't have to wait to hear the teaching: "God dwells within you as you." It will become your constant experience: *My God dwells within me.* You will experience oneness with your inner Self.

Truly, steady discipline is a precious gift.

MAY 25, 1997
Shree Muktananda Ashram
South Fallsburg, New York

CHAPTER 6

LET
your
HEART SING

THOUSANDS OF YEARS AGO, the sages of the *Rig Veda* sang these praises to God:

> Like the cry of watchful birds swimming in the water,
> like the loud claps of thundering rain clouds,
> like joyful streams gushing from the mountain,
> so do our hymns sound forth to the Lord.[1]

The impulse to sing for God is as ancient as the universe itself. Many cultures have been kept alive through the power of singing. In the very early days, this is how wisdom was preserved and passed down from generation to generation— through singing. Singing in praise of God is an intrinsic part of every being, every religious tradition.

Why has this practice endured through the ages? What is the secret? The answer is quite fascinating. Although the singer uses his voice to glorify God, it is the singer himself who receives the greatest benefit. Sing and see what happens to your heart. Sing and see what happens to your very being. The one who offers a song of love to God tastes a nectarean fruit. Singing opens the heart and makes paradise manifest. They say when someone is crying, sing to them. When difficulties come before you, sing to them. Singing removes barriers and invites you into a greater world. Singing in praise of God connects one place to another, one heart to another. It uplifts your spirits. You receive a fresh spirit. In Siddha Yoga meditation, this joyful sound is known as chanting.

Chanting is one of the most effective ways of becoming absorbed in God's presence. Chanting is a joyful meditation on God. Chanting reveals the courage in your own heart. It rings with contentment. Chanting is one of the key factors in imbibing the message *Wake up to your inner courage and become steeped in divine contentment.*

WHEN WE CHANT, we sing the names of God to classical Indian melodies known as ragas. Each raga evokes a particular mood. The notes are chosen and combined in such a way that they draw you very deep inside. They take you deep into meditation, into the mood of the particular raga. These ragas evoke great feelings when they are sung. Sometimes you wonder where these beautiful feelings have been hiding inside you. And when these melodies are combined with the names of God, tremendous power is generated within you.

As you repeat these names of God again and again, great devotion is released in your heart. These syllables are very powerful. They touch different parts of your being. It may take a little time to go deep into the womb of the chant, but wait—it does happen. A shift takes place. When that shift happens, it really happens, and you just know it. You become completely intoxicated. Being in this body becomes entirely comfortable.

Most of the time everyone is absolutely uncomfortable in this body. No one is really happy with his or her body. "I'm too fat!" "I'm too thin!" "I'm too tall." "I'm too short." "I'm beautiful." "I'm ugly." "Oh, I can be better. I should be more like that person." "Oh, look at her hair. It looks so much better than mine." "Oh, I ate too much. I really ate too much. I can't believe I ate so much. My stomach is bursting." "Oh, my pillow is too soft. I've got a cramp in my neck." No one is comfortable in this body.

But if you chant the name of God and allow yourself to be totally suffused with the light of God, this very body becomes a temple. Every little thing that bothered you about your physical being, every little thing that made you uncomfortable about the way you are, about the way you talk, about the way you laugh, about the way you cry, about the way you sleep, about the way you get up—it all changes. Somehow, everything has beauty and grace; everything has a mesmerizing quality like that of nature. Instead of being self-absorbed in an egotistical way, you rise above all that. You begin to understand what God has given you: your body, your life, and everything that exists.

In Siddha Yoga meditation, we don't set out to change the world. We are not asking anyone to change his religion. We are not asking anyone to change her family life or lifestyle. No. We have not set out to change the world in that way. But we have set out in this world to make people become aware that God is in everything. Wherever you are, you can experience God right there in that very moment. When this awareness increases, then whatever you do, you are able to reproduce the love of God. You come from that place.

BABA MUKTANANDA LOVED TO CHANT. It seemed that Baba found an opportunity every day to speak about the glory of chanting. Once he said:

> Chanting the name of God is yoga. It has great shakti. That shakti stills the mind and fills the heart

with love. Chanting destroys worry and pain and creates joy. It purifies the atmosphere both within and without. It kills the germs of restlessness in the mind. Whoever chants God's name with enthusiasm is filled with divine bliss.[2]

Baba puts it so clearly. "It kills the germs of restlessness in the mind."

Baba's words have a very contemporary significance. These days, everyone is so busy. You try to do so many things at once. With the information superhighway, every moment pulses with a staggering amount of business. Whether it's the world of computers, e-mail, faxes, and cell phones, or the world of TV and sound bites, everything is moving so fast. For what? Communication. This is the age of communication. There are seminars on communication. There are theories on the art of communication. Everyone is communicating these days.

With whom are you communicating? What connectedness do you feel with all these communications? With whom are you truly connecting? Where do you feel united? When do you experience the bliss of union? You are like a horse that starts out trotting, then cantering, then galloping, then galloping faster, then galloping faster and faster until you are racing flat out as though knees are digging into your ribs and spurs are cutting into your flanks. But who is whipping you? Who is whipping you into this frenzy? Who?

So many households are running to keep up with themselves. So many businesses are rat races. Think about it. With all this happening, who has time? Who has time to listen to the wind sweep through a canyon, to listen to an ailing palm tree or the silent song a pebble sings on the pavement? Who has time to help the poor or to feel the burden the earth carries?

Who has time to notice the silent tears of a hungry bird or to hear the silence of the desert? Who has time to listen to the prayer of jasmine flowers or to relish the delicious grapes of the vineyard? Who makes time to watch the moon rising, to behold the sunrise and the sunset?

Who has time to hear the affectionate words of loved ones, to listen as a little child talks about her time in school, or even to listen to the sound of your own breath? Who makes time to sit with the elders by the campfire, hearing the old stories and praising God? Who has time to hear the sweet music God whispers when you fall asleep at night?

You don't have time for this, do you? You are so busy, so very busy. Isn't that true?

Oddly enough, even with all the "busy-ness" of life, every person still finds time to worry. In an attempt to overcome this mounting tension, a person adds even more to his or her "to do" list. But then, the remedy moves even further away. The germs of restlessness of the mind become intolerable. Troubles pile up even higher than the clouds. Can't we put an end to this vicious cycle? Isn't there a way out?

Yes, there is. Just let the heart sing. Free up your time and chant! Chanting releases immense energy within you. It is astounding. It has the power to allow your sadness to surface. Then it wipes away the tears of sorrow and releases a fountain of joy. That is when your tears of sorrow become tears of joy.

Nagging thoughts do arise as you chant, only to be dissolved in the power of sound. Hidden feelings of unworthiness emerge from your heart, only to disintegrate in the power of sound. The discomforts of the mind and heart appear before you, only to say good-bye as the power of chanting takes hold of your heart. Even if anger comes up or pride sticks its head out, if fear is stalking you or jealousy is brewing, you just know these things no longer have a hold on your heart. They no longer shape your life.

IN REALITY, YOUR WHOLE BEING is made up of joy. The Upanishads say:

> You are born of love, you live in love,
> and you merge into love.
> You are born of joy, you live in joy,
> and you merge into joy.

Your whole being is made up of great joy and ecstasy. Therefore, you are naturally pulled toward the power of chanting, the singing of the heart. This pull is very strong, so let your heart sing. Flow with the natural inclination of your heart, your very being.

There was a poet-saint named Mirabai, who lived in India in the sixteenth century. Before she became a saint, she was a queen. It wasn't easy for her to chant the name of God whenever she wanted because the king and the people of the court did not appreciate her behaving like a monk or a devotee. They wanted her to observe all the royal duties. And she was willing. At the same time, she wanted to chant Krishna's name. She felt inside her heart that she was married to Krishna, and chanting His name released great purity and energy. In one of her songs, she says:

Mira is intoxicated with God's love.
She has become so absorbed in Krishna's love
    that she roams through the streets
    singing God's praises and chanting His name.
No one can stop her, Mira says.
No one can criticize her or stand in her way.
Intoxicated with divine love,
    she sings the names of the Lord—
    Govinda, Gopala—in great ecstasy.

Through chanting, divine joy is released. Through chanting, your inner being is transformed. Through chanting, your surroundings are sanctified. Through chanting, your courage shines forth and you become steeped in divine contentment.

This is why Siddha Yoga students chant so much. They chant whenever they arrive in a new place. They chant when they are driving. In fact, chanting with a benevolent intention has become a magnificent tradition. People chant during the birth of a baby, before exams, at a wedding, to celebrate their success, to send good wishes, for solace at the bedside of a patient, to invoke grace at the time of death. On countless occasions you can chant. Anytime you don't know what to do, you can chant. People ask, "What should I do when I begin my job?" Chant. "What should I do when I have to make a very important call?" Chant before you make the call. It totally changes your perception. You become filled with divine energy and great inspiration.

THERE WAS ONCE A KING named Akbar. He liked to ask his prime minister Birbal very difficult questions. One day he called Birbal and said to him, "Can you bring me the worst thing in this world?"

Birbal nodded his head. "Tomorrow, Your Majesty."

The next day when Birbal came before the king, the king asked him, "Have you brought the worst thing in the world?"

"Yes, Your Majesty," and he pointed to his tongue.

The king was curious. "Will you please explain yourself?"

"Your Majesty, this tongue is so wicked. It can say the worst things about people. It can wound so many hearts. It indulges in sweets and other delicious foods and makes the body sick. The tongue is the worst thing you can ever find in this world."

King Akbar was quite satisfied with that answer. Then he asked, "What about the best thing in the world? Can you bring me that?"

"Yes, Your Majesty. Tomorrow."

The next day when he approached, the king asked, "Have you brought the best thing in the world?"

"Yes, Your Majesty," and he pointed to his tongue.

This time, the king was very curious. "Can you please, once again, explain yourself?"

"Your Majesty, the tongue can say the best things about people. It can make everyone very happy. The tongue can speak so sweetly that it can heal the wounds of every heart. The tongue is precious. It is better than the best. It can control itself and make the whole body healthy. And moreover, this very tongue can chant God's name. It can praise God and make God's light manifest in everyone's life."

The tongue is the best thing you have. Use it to chant God's name. Baba used to say that chanting is a royal road to liberation. He had a unique way of emphasizing this point. He would say, "Chanting is a kind of insurance policy that guarantees God-realization, and anyone who doesn't chant won't enjoy this guarantee."[3]

It's a great insurance policy—chanting God's name. The power of chanting can transform your thinking, your understanding, and even your behavior. Let it enliven the way you do things, the way you look at things, the way you speak. Become fearless by taking refuge in the power of chanting.

DECEMBER 14, 1997
Palm Springs, California

CHANTING OPENS ALL DOORS. What kind of things do you discover when you chant? First of all, you come to know you can make a great sound. Imagine a sound filled with the sweetness of the heart. You can make that sound! A sound filled with God. You can hear in your voice the goodness in your heart. It's a great attainment. That alone should make you happy.

What are some of the other things you discover as you chant? Sound has the power to break down barriers. Chanting helps remove physical blockages within your body. Sometimes you may feel your breath is getting stuck, but when you give yourself to the chant, your breathing naturally becomes quite deep. Chanting creates a clear passageway.

When you befriend the practice of chanting, the body releases its tightness and tension. Then it can receive nourishment. Chanting nourishes the body. It is like drinking something nectarean, something you really love. It glides down your throat so wonderfully, and you are able to welcome it completely.

The syllables of the chants are sacred. Therefore, chanting can break down the barriers between you and your own heart. When the walls crumble, your heart shines forth like the morning sun, and then you know you have a great, giving heart. As long as you don't know what a great heart you have received from God, you always live in poverty-consciousness.

The joy of chanting unfurls the inner world. It is like the petals of a flower being revealed one by one. Just as a rose blossoms, your whole being flowers naturally with the power of chanting. You become filled with deep and unshakable contentment.

DECEMBER 21, 1997
Palm Springs, California

CHAPTER 7

MOVING OUT
of the
HOUSE OF LACKS

WE ARE POISED ON THE EVE of the winter solstice. This day marks the return of the light. Soon all of nature will be gathering its will to break through into spring. It is a time of ripening and quickening. I want to invite you to dive into the teachings. If you are just sitting on the edge, waiting for something to happen, I invite you to dive in. No matter who or what brought you here, dive in and have your own experience. You are here to have an inner journey, to perceive your own inner light. You are here to become anchored in the Truth, the supreme Consciousness, the perfect love within you.

When you stop and think about it, isn't it amazing? No matter how magnificent the inner world is, it usually goes unnoticed. It is like your heartbeat. You know your heartbeat goes on all the time and keeps your body alive. Without it, your body would no longer exist. Yet most people ignore this miracle. How often do you think about the heartbeat? How often do you experience the heart pulsing, pulsing, pulsing? Perhaps when you are in love or when someone is sick. But most of the time, are you aware of the heartbeat? Yet it is pulsing all the time.

What this shows is how unconscious and ungrateful human beings can become. And ingratitude can actually lead a person's life to disaster. Therefore, to hear the sound of your own heartbeat and to rediscover its magnificence is a boon. If a person doesn't even notice the heartbeat of the physical body, can it be any wonder that he is not aware of the inner world, the subtler realms?

A true seeker wants to see the inner light, to rediscover the magnificence of the Self, and to live in a constant state of gratitude. Sometimes people used to ask Baba Muktananda, "What is the best way to live my life?" Baba would say, "In gratitude." It's so simple. If you have gratitude, you have everything. The saints of every tradition have echoed this message.

One of these saints, Bhartrihari, was a great king in India. Later in his life, he renounced his kingdom and devoted all his time to seeking God and singing His praises. Bhartrihari writes:

> Wander no longer with weary footsteps
> > in the thickets of the senses.
> Instead, find that better way,
> > which will bring you freedom from all troubles
> > in a single instant.
> Unite yourself with the supreme Being
> > and abandon your current state,
> > which is as unstable as the waves of the sea.
> Turn away from things that distract you.
> O my heart, be calm! [1]

Bhartrihari entreats us to seek the inner world, to unite ourselves with that which gives life to all animate beings and inanimate objects. This is the supreme Self, the invisible matrix from which creation emerges. This universe is a perfect reflection of God, the universal soul. To live in harmony with God's creation is to live a life filled with grace. To turn within and experience your oneness with God is the fulfillment of all human endeavors.

WE HAVE BEEN DELVING DEEPLY into the message *Wake up to your inner courage and become steeped in divine contentment.* Bhartrihari says, "O my heart, be calm. Wander no longer with weary footsteps in the thickets of the senses." The senses are wonderful: through the eyes you can see, through the ears you can hear, through the hands you can touch. You need the senses to experience this world as fully as you truly want to. Nonetheless, think about how you use your eyes, how you use your ears, how you use your hands.

Many times when you use your senses, you are not even sure you like what you are doing. So with "weary footsteps" you live your life—but how much meaning is there in such a life? If you don't have a fresh spirit to do what you need to do, to go where you need to go, you drag through your days.

The incredible experience of contentment has been the divine invitation of the saints and sages throughout time. Their sublime thoughts have been passed like blazing torches from one great soul to another. For thousands of years, profound experiences have been recorded in the scriptures of every tradition. It is our great good fortune that they have been made available to us. We can read them; we can study them; we can practice them. We can make an attempt to live our lives by the light of these magnificent teachings.

The great beings point the way to the supreme Truth and show us how to live our lives accordingly. Only when you taste the highest bliss do you realize who has awakened that inner experience within you. Therefore, in gratitude, we say, *"Sadgurunāth mahārāj kī jay!"* Hail to the true Guru! Hail to the wonderful Guru, who lives in my own heart, who awakens my awareness, who kindles my heart!

The inner journey is the most rewarding quest you can ever undertake. At the same time, it is an arduous one. You come to know the great light within you, and you also encounter the unpleasant things that keep you from this light. To walk deep into your own being and still retain the highest respect for yourself is a wondrous attainment. This inward journey is our path; it is the path of meditation.

You may be unfamiliar with meditation, but your own breath will be your faithful companion. When you follow the breath, you are able to become still, and the path of meditation opens up for you. In the company of the breath, you can travel with ease to the place of contentment within yourself.

For a few moments now, focus your attention on your breath as it comes in and goes out. Consciously breathe in deep and breathe out long. You can scan the body to observe if there is any holding back. If there is, allow your body to relax even more. Continue to breathe in deep and breathe out long.

As you breathe deeply, very naturally your mind becomes still and quiet. Find the stillness in the breath.

Contentment lives in this stillness. Let the mind rest in the steady rhythm of the breath. Let the breath gently carry your mind to the ocean of contentment within. Wake up to your inner courage and become steeped in divine contentment.

Recently someone who practices Siddha Yoga meditation told me she loves what happens after she watches her breath for a while. She enters a deep state of contentment. When she is at a program and meditating with others, she is able to get into that state promptly. However, when she meditates at home, sometimes it takes her two hours to reach that beautiful state. But she is not discouraged, she said. If it takes two hours, she thinks it's fine. She has the whole day ahead, full of activities. So if she gets up early in the morning and sits for meditation and waits for that divine fruit of contentment—which comes when the breath is still, when the mind is still, when the whole world within and without is totally still—she says it is well worth it.

Some people experience the state of stillness very quickly. When this happens to you, cherish it. Hold on to it. Treasure it. Learn to feel gratitude for this experience. It is a great boon.

AS YOU DECIDE TO WAKE UP to your own inner courage, you come across discoveries that are quite surprising and at times disturbing. Some are habits you had no idea you were courting within yourself. Others are tendencies you thought you had overcome a long time ago. You think, "I'm looking for my courage! Why am I being pounded down by these horrible misgivings about myself? I'm trying to become steeped in divine contentment. Why am I suddenly plagued by restlessness and panic?"

Well, when you set out on a journey, you do come across the unexpected. For example, let's say your goal is to find exceptional pearls in the ocean. Before you reach your destination, you have to cut through miles and miles of tangled seaweed. You encounter predators of every size and shape, who have claimed the reef as their territory. Who are you to intrude?

However, since you are determined to arrive at your goal,

you make every effort to dodge them, to get rid of them, to make your way around them, to go beyond them, or even to befriend them. Whatever it takes, you will do it. You won't give up and let yourself sink to the bottom. You won't sputter with indignation, "Well, no one told me that before I got the pearls this was going to happen!" Instead, you keep diving for the treasure. Until you have the pearls in hand, your destination draws you like a magnet. An incredible driving force within you keeps you going, no matter what.

In the same way, when you are on the spiritual path of inner discovery, don't turn back the minute you meet an obstacle or the minute things don't go your way. When you are waking up to your inner courage, don't abandon your strength the moment you encounter a challenge. You can't let little things catch you off guard or stop you dead in your tracks. Fear can deprive you of your own great life.

On the spiritual path, you can't let every groundless fear paralyze you or fill you with discouragement. When you complain, when you get angry, when you are miffed, what is happening? You are discouraged, you feel hopeless, you are frustrated, you lose your contentment. And then what happens? What happens to your physical body? What happens to your spirits when you let yourself get discouraged and feel hopeless? You lose so much.

So what if a gigantic log falls across your path with a crash that sounds like thunder? So what if a tiny mouse squeaks at you? Baba used to say, "Have courage. Don't get dysentery whenever a mouse squeaks at you." This was one of his favorite lines; he used to say it all the time.

You must keep going. If you abandon your purpose, fear and discontent will haunt you. But when you wake up to your inner courage, you won't let anything stand in the way. You will find your priceless inner treasure—divine contentment. As Bhartrihari says, "O my heart, be calm."

ONCE SOMEONE ASKED BABA MUKTANANDA, "How can I stop comparing myself with others and remain contented with my life?" Baba replied:

> Why should you go around comparing yourself with others? Why don't you try to attain awareness of the inner Self, which is the creator of all, and become anchored in that awareness? If there is anything you should compare yourself with, it is your own inner Self, your own Consciousness. Only then will you attain stability.[2]

Baba's answers constantly bring your attention back to your own divine Consciousness. When you have stability, when you have contentment, you are able to enjoy your merits. Without contentment, you lose everything. It doesn't matter how bright you are, how strong you are, how well educated or generous you are; it doesn't matter how rich or poor you are. When you don't have inner contentment, you lose your merits. You are always counting someone else's blessings. You drive yourself crazy counting all the things you lack. Will there ever be an end to your lacks?

In this way, you lose sight of the goal and everything in between. You build yourself an entire house of lacks. Poor house, it can barely stand. It keeps collapsing on top of you, and you suffer terribly. In spite of this, you rebuild your flimsy house of lacks again and again. But like a house of straw, one tiny spark of jealousy and it all goes up in flames. Haven't you noticed?

When you live in a house of lacks, this is what it's like: "I'm not getting enough love. I'm not getting enough money. I'm not getting enough education. I'm not getting enough property. I'm not getting enough rest. I'm not getting enough attention. I'm not getting enough spiritual experiences."

This is a story I have heard many times over the years. You have a spiritual experience. It is awesome, magnificent, wonderful, splendid, and at that moment you say, "If nothing else ever happens to me, I don't care. This is the experience of all experiences! Now I know the path is valid, the Guru is true, the teachings are right."

Then you find out someone else also had an amazing experience, and what's more, that person knows how to articulate it so well! What happens? You get discouraged and you think, "I'm not a good meditator. I'm not a good chanter. Well, Baba never loved me anyway. I probably fantasized that he did. People told me I was just making it all up, and maybe they were right. All I need is one more spiritual experience. Then for sure I will know this path is true. Then I will know that what the swamis are saying is true." Your mind carries on in this way.

So you have another experience and you say, "Oh, I'm so fortunate. I'm so content. O Guruji, I'll hold on to your feet for the rest of my life! I will give my life to seva! What is life for, after all? It's for service!"

But then you go to a meditation program. After chanting and meditation, a speaker stands up, and with full fanfare he says, "I was in this deep blue ocean, and there I met God face to face. He smiled at me, and I melted in that smile. I was absorbed into His being. There was nothing left of me but the deep blue ocean of God. Now I know that I am God, I am God!"

And you think, "Hmmm." One spark of jealousy, and it all goes up in flames.

Do you know what is so ironic about all this? Your merits are turned to ashes, but the lacks are not burned up. Your virtues are destroyed, but your discontent grows out of control. Because you spend so much time grasping at what you don't have, your hands can only hold unfulfilled desires. They are not open to receive the countless blessings, the abundance of grace. Contentment becomes a myth.

How do you find a better place to live? How can you gain the courage to move out of this familiar world of discontent? How do you abandon the house of lacks? Remember what Baba said: Attain stability. If you must compare yourself with something or someone, then compare yourself with divine Consciousness. Go for the highest; go for the best. By observing the splendor of the Self, you attain stability. Be still and become anchored in your own heart.

The magnificence of your heart cannot be compared with anything in this world. When your heart is open, when you are in your heart, the way you perceive the sunrise, the trees, the mountains is extraordinary; it is unique. Thousands of people may see the same thing you see, but if they are not in touch with the heart, they may not feel what you feel. What does this show? Consciousness blazes in its fullness in the heart. Of course, Consciousness pulsates in the mountains, in the desert, in the trees, in the animals, in the birds, in water, in fire. Consciousness is everywhere. Nonetheless, it is in the heart that it blazes in its fullness. So again and again, bring your attention back to the magnificence of your heart. When your heart experiences contentment, know that God is present.

THE OTHER MORNING I was contemplating the existence of divine light. I was thinking about the way we go to sleep and wake up. The cycle continues as long as this body is alive. However, the divine light never stops; it is never extinguished. It is perpetually awake in its most brilliant and tender form. It vibrates in both its visible and invisible form. When the sun rises, we say it is daytime. The light makes everything glisten. The world becomes apparent because of its radiance. Then when the sun sets, we say it is nighttime. However, the divine light doesn't come and go: the light that exists in the sun is present in the moon and in the stars. It also exists in trees and planets and the wind. The divine light is unceasingly alive in every particle of Consciousness. It is in tune with the universal soul. The deathless, immortal light that pulsates with knowledge exists in everything.

As I contemplated this divine light, I was wonderstruck at its incredible beauty, its purity, its simplicity, its grandeur, its humility, and its generosity. This miraculous light is beyond the reach of mind and speech. Yet it is the source of inspiration for all forms of expression.

A few minutes later I happened to open a book of contemplations, where I came upon a wonderful passage about the loom of life and how it never stops weaving. The pattern that is weaving when the sun goes down is still weaving when the sun comes up the next morning.

Isn't it the same thing with your own being? The loom of life creates so many textures: You may be awake or asleep. You may think you are happy or sad. You may feel that you have achieved great things in life or that there is nothing you can ever achieve. You may believe that you have everything you need, or that you are unlucky and always empty-handed. However, beneath all these fluctuations, the divine light constantly shimmers within and without. It maintains the order of the universe.

Through meditation, you become aware of this divine light. When you let yourself become quiet, when you settle into the breath, you find yourself in the heart. This is the amazing experience that happens when you sit for meditation. As you become accustomed to this practice, you can simply sit on your *āsana*, your meditation mat, and walk into your own heart, the subtle heart, the innermost core of your being. To discover the divine splendor of this heart is the purpose of life, the goal of the inner journey. This heart is the wellspring of courage and contentment.

Someone once asked Baba Muktananda, "Could you reveal some secret about penetrating one's heart?"

Baba replied, "That is what meditation is for. Shaktipat and meditation are meant precisely for penetrating the heart. You go within; you focus the mind and lead it toward the heart."[3]

Notice there is a sweet effort involved here: taking the mind to the heart. Baba went on to say, "It is something very great if you can enter the heart. It is the most important center; there is no other center that can be compared with the heart."[4]

I love the way Baba put things; he made it all very simple, direct, and profound: "That is what meditation is for." He spoke with such freedom—he spoke from the scriptures, about the scriptures, and from his own experiences. He made it all wonderfully accessible. Just being with him was a beautiful sadhana. To this day, you can look at his picture and you know you are looking into purity. You can look at his picture and you know you are in meditation. Even if you cannot meditate, just look at his picture before you go to work. Your whole day will be different. He will come to you. In fact, he will go with you to work.

It is something very great if you can enter the heart.

THERE IS A BEAUTIFUL *bhajan* Baba loved to sing. It is by the poet-saint Tikadas who lived in northern India.

> The Lord permeates every cell of my body.
> When He is so close to me,
>   why should I go anywhere else to find Him?
> He is fathomless, endless, invisible, and eternal.
> He delights the minds of noble people.
> The scriptures are unable to encompass His greatness.
> He is the abode of *sacchidānanda*:
> Existence, Consciousness, and Bliss Absolute.
> Tika says, My Guru is *nirañjana*, supremely pure.
> Being in the shelter of his grace, I feel sanctified,
>   and I experience the divinity of my own being.
> The Lord permeates every cell of my body.

"The Lord permeates every cell of my body. When He

is so close to me, why should I go anywhere else to find Him?" That is exactly what happens when you meditate on the breath, when you meditate on the Lord within, on the divine light—you discover Him inside.

In Siddha Yoga, meditation happens spontaneously through grace. In the shelter of the Guru's grace, you are able to experience the light of your heart, the sanctity of your own being. As the breath moves in and out, you become aware of the divine light within and without. Beneath the fluctuations of everything in your life, there is something very stable, concrete, and ever present. It is the divine light, which is unceasingly alive in every particle of Consciousness.

Take a moment now and become aware of your breathing. Have the awareness: *I am light. I am Consciousness.* Beneath all the fluctuations of the mind, the divine light constantly shimmers. It is the foundation of your whole being.

I am light. I am Consciousness. This divine light never sleeps. It is perpetually awake, brilliant, tender, pure, and generous, illumining the mind, illumining the heart.

I am light. I am Consciousness. When you watch the sunrise, the beautiful shimmering sun, you can breathe in the sun and breathe out the sun. Have this experience—breathing in the sun and breathing out the sun. Visualize the rising sun. All its colors are beautiful, tender, healing, mesmerizing. Breathe in the sun; breathe out the sun.

Discover the splendor of your heart. It is shimmering with divine light. It is the wellspring of courage and contentment. Let the sun permeate your entire being. Let your whole body shimmer with this divine light. Let the warm glow of the sun relax your mind; let the warm glow relax your body.

As Baba said, lead your mind to the heart. Breathe in the sun; breathe out the sun. Let your whole being melt into the light of the sun. Within and without—one great light. The light is full inside the body. The light is full outside the body. The barrier of the body dissolves and becomes one with divine light. Let your whole being shimmer with divine light.

Rest in the contentment of divine light.

WAKE UP TO YOUR INNER COURAGE and become steeped in divine contentment. You have come here to make an inner journey. You have come here to discover the light within. You are here to become anchored to the supreme Truth in your heart. Carry on with your journey no matter how many obstacles or challenges you face. Have courage. Rest in the contentment of the divine light.

Thank you for being here in your own heart. Whenever I thank you, it isn't for anything you have done externally. It is because you have taken time, you have put forth effort to know your own heart, to be with your heart, to see your heart, to become anchored in your heart. When you are in touch with your heart, I am truly able to say thank you. And this "thank you" isn't a mere formality: it comes from our oneness. Thank you for being here with your hearts so sweet and full of longing, so full of wanting to know, just to know. Thank you, each one of you. Thank you.

DECEMBER 20, 1997
Palm Springs, California

WHEN YOU FINALLY SAY GOOD-BYE to insecurities, negativities, and uncertainties, you feel so much freedom. This decision doesn't require a dramatic speech. It's very simple. You just make the firm decision not to be tied to a drab life, not to be controlled by fear and its offshoots like bad habits, meanness, and suspicion. When you do this, you will find so much more space in your being. Ah, you can breathe again! There is more space for the splendor of God. More space for good thoughts. Your good thoughts don't have to be squeezed out of you; they can dance out of you!

When you finally make the decision that you will no longer be led around by negativities, you will feel such freedom. The feeling of bondage will disappear. Inner blocks will be released as the divine *kundalinī shakti* flows through your system.

When you decide once and for all that you will not allow adversities to overwhelm you or dictate your opinion of yourself and the rest of the world, you will feel lighter. You will feel glorious. The joy of fearlessness is a great reminder of the splendor of God and the blessings that abound in your life.

Truly, when you are fearless, you can hear celestial music ringing in every cell of your body. Your body becomes an exquisite musical instrument through which God breathes and plays and dances! Then, wherever you go, you bring a ray of hope. Those in the grip of sorrow brighten up. Your presence actually becomes the splendor of God. Everything you do creates an atmosphere of well-being on this planet, both within and without.

So why don't you make a commitment to yourself to remember the joy of fearlessness. Make a beautiful resolution to recover the awareness of the splendor of God. If you do, you will begin to see all the blessings that are continually unfolding in your life.

DECEMBER 28, 1996
Shree Muktananda Ashram
South Fallsburg, New York

CHAPTER 8

BE STEADFAST, EMBRACE
your own
INNER COURAGE

HERE IN THE DESERT, we have been watched over by the powerful presence of the San Jacinto Mountains. We have seen the mountains adorned with the golden light of the morning sun. We have viewed them dressed in moonlight and rainbows and clouds of every description. In every mood, their majestic presence resounds with one message for us: *Wake up to your inner courage and become steeped in divine contentment.* This message is itself a mountain of grace, and it endows us with a great reminder: Be steadfast, embrace your own inner courage.

Life sends us all countless invitations to embrace our courage. Could a baby stand up and take its first steps without courage? Could a child enter a schoolroom full of strangers for the first time without courage? Could a young adult go for his first job interview without courage? And doesn't it take a courageous heart to sit beside an elderly person who is dying? Even the quietest, most sedate life obliges you to call on the courage of your heart, not just once, but many times. Life compels you again and again to ascend to uncharted territory. No one can do it for you. You must have courage within. It is *your* courage.

And what role does steadfastness play? How necessary is steadfastness? Imagine climbing a mountain and being suspended on the sheer rock face of a cliff. What makes you persist? Or if you don't want to go that far, think of climbing a tree or a tall ladder. Or think of walking on a tightrope stretched between two cliffs. You are committed; you are way out there and a wind rises. Your balance is shaky. You have gone too far to go back, and the wind is picking up, getting rougher. Now, at such a moment, what can you do?

There is only one answer: pick a steady point at your destination and fasten your attention there. Hold on strong. The point of balance is inside you. What will save you is the wholeness of your focus on the goal and your willingness to keep going. What will save you is steadfastness. At times like that, you just can't waver, you can't wobble, you have to be strong. Everyone will give you this advice. But what are they really saying? Basically, they are telling you to wake up to your inner resources and value them. Live them. Rely on them. They are saying, Be steadfast, embrace your own inner courage.

Life is full of critical moments, and sooner or later you come to realize one thing: you have to hold fast to what you believe in, what is yours to offer, what you must accomplish, and what you want to be. Each one of you knows this instinctively. To bring anything to completion, you need the power of steadfastness. As the Spanish proverb says, *El que persevera, alcanza:* He who perseveres reaches the goal.

STEADFASTNESS LITERALLY MEANS adhering firmly and devotedly to something. You become fastened to something; you become established in it. Steadfastness implies that you are dedicated, intent, and faithful, that you are unswerving, unflinching, and undistracted.

On the spiritual path, steadfastness has even more meanings. It is the attainment that makes all other attainments possible. But to understand steadfastness, you have to make a giant leap. Just thinking about it isn't enough. How can one understand steadfastness? It is quite subtle. When you are climbing a mountain, you have something very solid and tangible to hold on to. But on the spiritual journey, your supports seem to be invisible. They don't register on the physical plane; the senses can't really pick them up. And with nothing concrete to hang on to, it is very easy to get caught in the quagmire of the mind. It can be a real swamp. On the one hand, there are doubts, which can be like swimming in mud. On the other hand, there is becoming dogmatic, which can be just as much of a mess.

Have you ever come up against the danger of being dogmatic about the teachings? Sometimes people hear: "Be steadfast, embrace your inner courage. Be steadfast in your practice." And they run with it in the wrong direction. For instance, in our Siddha Yoga meditation ashrams, there is a beautiful daily schedule. This schedule was handcrafted by Baba Muktananda to balance all the spiritual practices and allow seekers to make the most of their time in the ashram. A Siddha Yoga meditation ashram is like an eternal retreat site where people come and devote their time fully to spiritual practices. They absorb the divine energy of the practices in the ashram, and then they take that energy home. The daily schedule allows you to get up very early in the morning. Before dawn there is the morning *āratī* and meditation, followed by chanting of the *Guru Gītā*. Then there is breakfast, seva, the noon chant, then lunch, rest, afternoon seva, evening *āratī*, dinner, the evening chant, and to bed at an early hour. This ashram schedule is a thing of beauty. It is one of Baba's masterpieces.

However, in the name of steadfastness, some people try to cram the entire ashram schedule into their work, home, and family schedule. Is that steadfastness in yoga? No. How can you tell? Because you collapse in one way or another. You feel guilty or your work suffers. You begin to hate your practices. Or your spouse. Or perhaps both. The mind can get lost in the bog of wrong understanding. Steadfastness is subtler than that.

You have to find a realistic way of doing sadhana in your daily life. "Choose one or two of your favorite practices," Baba used to say, "and do them regularly." Give full attention to whatever you are doing and do it at a harmonious pace. Your own schedule and the schedule of your family—both are important.

Now there are people who diet to death or exercise to death in the name of steadfastness. They think they are being extremely steadfast. But this is called compulsion, my dear ones, not steadfastness.

HOW CAN YOU DISCOVER this amazing quality—steadfastness? It is a difficult one to understand right off the bat. On the one hand, you don't want to be as stiff as a board. On the other hand, you don't want to be like loose rocks on a mountainside that roll all the way downhill at the slightest disturbance. True steadfastness sparkles with flexibility. It brings out the best in you. It anchors you in goodness.

Can we eliminate any other misconceptions about this virtue called steadfastness? Steadfastness is that middle ground, the perfect balance. Does this imply perfect discipline? Well, steadfastness is not just about performing daily duties regularly without fail. It is not about punctuality. These are good qualities, unquestionably, and very helpful in your life. But they are not what we mean when we speak about steadfastness from the viewpoint of spirituality. To understand this essential quality, we began with a process of elimination. We have been saying steadfastness is not this, it's not that; it's not found here, it doesn't exist there. Bit by bit, we will get clearer about the true meaning and value of steadfastness.

Where does steadfastness come from and how can we attain it? Steadfastness is *antarsthiti*, an inner state. It has no outer support. It is not easily identified. Other virtues like generosity and humility have much more obvious outer expressions. In generosity, for example, there is giving. You can see and identify that quality. Genuine humility is also quite unmistakable. But with steadfastness there is no outward display, and therefore you might not receive immediate compliments for it. Steadfastness is the inner pillar. You are the strength. You are the mountain of courage.

Your breath has true steadiness. Despite all the ups and downs in life, the breath still comes in and goes out, comes in and goes out. You may be crying, still the breath is moving. You may be laughing, still the breath is moving. You are awake, and the breath is moving. You are asleep, and the breath is moving. You are happy, the breath is moving. You are angry, the breath is moving. You don't like this world, the breath is still moving. You love this world, the breath keeps on moving. It is so steady. The steadfastness of the breath is what keeps you alive. It is such a reliable friend. Through the breath, you can experience your own strength.

Recently someone gave me a printout of a computer image of the rib cage and diaphragm. One image showed how they look in the full inhale position, and the other in the full exhale position. The ribs were a silvery gray color, and through the ribs you could see a dash of rosy red, which was the diaphragm. This picture of the rib cage was beautiful, really mesmerizing. The image made a great point—there is something glowing inside your rib cage. As you breathe in and breathe out, remember that the same pinkish red glow of the sunrise is also inside your rib cage.

WHEN I THINK OF STEADFASTNESS, I think of Baba. He was the personification of steadfastness. Once someone asked him, "Is it all right to pray to the Guru for help in difficulties?"

Baba replied, "It is all right to pray to the Guru for help in difficulties, but it is better to turn your difficulties into nectar, and then try to digest that nectar with great joy. It is very valuable, very important to digest your own difficulties."[1]

"Turn your difficulties into nectar"—what a teaching from Baba! What a sublime command. The answer is worth your whole life, and it gives a key to what steadfastness in yoga really is. It is the process of releasing inner nectar, and it is born out of spiritual practices. Spiritual practice is what makes steadfastness come alive.

Steadfastness means you hold on to God's love no matter what is happening in your life. You fasten your mind to God's love, to the Truth. You fasten your mind to the divine energy, to *kundalinī shakti*, the great force. This inner force is unassailable. You fasten your mind with all your might to the feet of the Lord. If everything revolves around the Lord, like a wheel around its hub, then you are in the experience of steadfastness all the time. You are completely anchored inside.

This is what steadfastness on the spiritual path means—fastening your mind to inner wisdom. It is holding on to the lifegiving energy as situations arise and dissolve, arise and subside, come and go. Steadfastness is the inner pillar that turns difficulties into nectar.

You hear the echo of this unswerving determination and intent in the poetry of many saints. This is the secret they share through their prayers. Through the most agonizing circumstances, the poet-saint Mirabai kept the flame of God alive in her heart. She was so steadfast that nothing could divert her gaze from the feet of her Lord. She writes, "O my beloved Krishna, dye my shawl in Your own color." Although the shawl represents the body, Mirabai is talking about her very being: "O Krishna, dye my entire being in Your own color. Dye my heart in the color of Your love."

This unwavering focus on God is what saints of all traditions pray for. A famous poem by Saint Teresa of Avila expresses perfect steadfastness. You can sense the years of practice in every phrase. You can feel the understanding she extracted from the difficulties in her life. This poem is nectar.

> Let nothing perturb you, nothing frighten you.
> All things pass.
> God never changes.
> Patience achieves everything.
> Whoever has God lacks nothing.
> God alone suffices.
> *Sólo Dios basta.*[2]

If you hold a bar of gold in your hand, you feel wealthy and financially secure. You know you can call on it wherever you go and its value will always be recognized. Similarly, when your mind is fixed on the Lord, on God's love, on serving the Truth, it gives you unusual assurance. You have a deep confidence and unearthly strength. It is an inner security fund that will always be there for you when you need it.

Without this focus, even intelligent and talented people cave in the moment a difficulty arises. They just don't know how to handle it because they don't know where to place their trust. They have never practiced placing their trust in that which never changes.

Saint Teresa says, "God never changes." The *Bhagavad Gītā* says the supreme Self is immutable. Or you could say, learn to place your trust in that which is glowing inside your rib cage. Be steadfast and embrace your own courage.

THE POET-SAINT JNANESHWAR MAHARAJ says, "Steadfastness is that courage through which a person would not close his eye of clear perception even if the heavens were to fall."[3]

This kind of steadfastness is made manifest through one thing and one thing only—and that is practice. I know you are waiting for something special, some magical formula, and here it is! Anyone who has done the practices wholeheartedly knows how magical, how nectarean they are. You sit for meditation, and the mantra churns up all kinds of things inside you: divine thoughts, not-so-divine thoughts, sublime thoughts, not-so-sublime thoughts. But no matter what is stirred up, you patiently bring your mind back to the name of God. Sometimes when people close their eyes for meditation, they see images, they have visions. Some of these they like and some they don't like so much. It doesn't really matter what the images are; you keep your mind focused on God's love. You practice steadfastness. You bring your mind back to the name of God. As a lover of God has said:

O Lord, may Your name be on my lips.
May I meditate on You
    in the morning and in the evening.
May I always remember You
    incessantly day and night.
May my mind always be fixed on Your feet.

Whatever arises, you open your heart to God's energy as it washes through your mind. You give yourself to meditation. And each time you perform this act of worship, another grain of steadfastness is added to your storehouse of virtues.

Baba Muktananda speaks about steadfastness from his own experience. He says: Strength flows through your whole being after you enthrone God in your heart. This strength is the power of the inner Self, and it is most sublime.[4]

Just imagine enthroning God in your heart! When you have a beautiful possession, you want to put it in the ideal place, somewhere safe and pure. So imagine finding a place for God. Where would you place the Lord? What would be the perfect place? Enthrone God in your heart, says Baba, and great strength flows through your entire being.

When you place a beautiful possession in the perfect spot, it looks just right and you enjoy its beauty. Everyone who comes to your house admires it. But it doesn't increase your strength. It doesn't enhance your virtues. However, when you enthrone God in your heart, you receive so much. You receive everything you are looking for. Divine energy washes through you. When you enthrone God in your heart, strength flows in your whole being. Then you are able to approach all challenges courageously, with an attitude dipped in the nectar of the teachings. You are able to probe all situations with your grace-filled intellect and maintain the clear eye of perception that Jnaneshwar speaks about. You are able to distill any difficulties that confront you. Then you can drink the nectar they contain and let it nourish you with its wisdom. As Baba said, "Turn your difficulties into nectar." You can do this with steadfastness. And by doing this, you attain even more steadfastness.

Enthrone God in your heart. Allow your entire being to become drenched in God's love. Totally trust God's love and live from that place. Then, without even knowing it, you become steadfast, you embrace your own inner courage.

DECEMBER 27, 1997
Palm Springs, California

AS A STUDENT ON THE SPIRITUAL PATH, you have embarked on an extraordinary adventure. You may not be dwelling in a Himalayan cave. You may not be living with a Guru and just two other disciples in a remote corner of this world. You may not have taken the vows of *brahmacharya* or *sannyāsa*, vows in which you give your life completely to serving God. Nonetheless, you are on a spiritual path; you are doing sadhana. And this path blazes with the fire of *kundalinī shakti*. Whoever walks on this path is purified. And when a person is being purified, many things happen to the body, mind, and emotions. All kinds of transformations take place.

Some people have dramatic experiences; others have very subtle ones. Sometimes the process is very physical and obvious; sometimes it is extremely subtle. And sometimes this process of *kundalinī* unfolding happens at such a deep level inside that you don't even know it is happening until years later. You look back and say, "I feel so different. I feel great. My life has been completely transformed."

In the course of your life, you do so many things. Whatever you are doing, whether you are quietly contemplating the teachings or putting them into action, whether you are going to sleep with the awareness of the teachings or remembering them while you cook, whether you bring the teachings into the air so they can shine when others are fighting or you just hum the teachings to yourself as you take a walk, it is very important that you allow the fountain of knowledge to spring forth continually from within. This is the true bath, the true ritual—constantly allowing yourself to bathe in the fountain of knowledge that springs forth from within.

Of course, sometimes you are sad, and sometimes you are shrouded in dilemmas. Sometimes you are completely involved with difficulties, and yet at other times full of ecstasy. These variations will be there. No one says you should not be experiencing them. No one says that if you have such experiences, you are a victim or a horrible person or unenlightened. It does not mean you have a long way to go or you are not a spiritual person or you are not a noble person. No. You are noble. You are enlightened. You are spiritual. You are considerate and kind. You are a virtuous person. You are a true human being when you allow yourself to bathe in the fountain of knowledge that springs forth from within. And you have that knowledge within you. You do.

Over and over again, people on this path have shared the most classical and extraordinary experiences that reflect incredible knowledge. Where do these experiences come from? They come from the fountain of knowledge that springs forth from within all the time.

This knowledge arises from inside. So come into this inner place, come into your true abode.

If you find that you are afraid of intense spiritual experiences, the kind that Baba Muktananda describes in *Play of Consciousness*, go ahead: feel as much fear as you want to. If you are doubting such experiences, that's fine: doubt them to your heart's fill. Doubt them fully. If you are agitated by the thought of intense experiences, then be agitated. Embrace your agitation. If you are angry about such experiences, go ahead and be angry.

Remember, you are here in this life to do sadhana and to understand something more than you have known before. You are here to take with you something more than you have known so far. Greatness exists like an ocean within you. Why do you want to act like a fish out of water, wriggling on the sand under the scorching sun? Look! The water is just one millimeter away! Jump in!

You should understand that this path is the blazing fire of *kundalinī shakti*. The crusts of impurity fall away. This path is not for fainthearted people. This path is for the courageous.

JUNE 29, 1997
Shree Muktananda Ashram
South Fallsburg, New York

CHAPTER 9

A MOUNTAIN
of
STEADINESS

WHEN YOU OBSERVE THE MOUNTAINS, when you watch the moon rise or the sun set, you experience a sweet and wondrous silence. You want to savor it again and again. Is there a way to recreate this silence without going to the mountains, without watching the moon rise, without being anywhere special? Just being where you are?

Yes, there is. Every time you have satsang, every time you gather together to be in the company of the Truth, of divine knowledge, you are able to create the same sweet and wondrous silence. In this silence you grow spiritually. Because of it, your devotion expands. What brings about such silence? It is the power of good company, the power of meditation, the power of the mantra, the power of chanting that create this sweet and most extraordinary silence. And when you are able to hear this silence in the air, you experience your own steadfastness.

BABA MUKTANANDA BROUGHT the tradition of the Indian scriptures to the West. In fact, Baba brought the Indian scriptures to life for many, many people. One of these scriptures, the ancient *Sāma Veda*, says:

> O courageous one, who strives after the expansive life, go forward, face opposition, overcome obstacles. Your inner force is unassailable. You will certainly attain prosperity. Slay your ignorance with your strength. Have mastery over all your actions!

Baba would often repeat this: "Have mastery over all your

actions. Become the master of your senses." Speaking about this inner force, Baba also said:

> It is very important for a human being to awaken his *kundalini*. It is a power, a vibration, an extraordinary energy. It is the soul of an individual and his vital force. It is the conscious power behind his senses. It is that which inspires the intellect and makes the mind contemplate. Siddha Yoga teaches that this entire universe is pervaded by the great shakti.[1]

Over and over again Baba loved to say: "This entire universe is pervaded by the great shakti." His words about the shakti are direct and potent. When *kundalini shakti* is awakened within, a most significant inner attainment takes place: you are able to become steadfast and embrace your inner courage. You become a mountain of steadiness.

What a great boon it is to be steadfast in this transitory world where everything changes. In the blink of an eye, events form and dissolve. At times, daily life feels like a bed of quicksand. Baba constantly warned seekers not to invest their life in the ephemeral things of this world.

Once someone arrived in Gurudev Siddha Peeth with a special gift for Baba—the latest-model flashlight. As Baba examined the gift, the person said, "Baba, it has a lifetime guarantee."

Baba looked at it very carefully and then asked with a smile, "It's guaranteed for whose lifetime—mine, or the flashlight's?"

Attaining steadfastness in this fleeting world is no ordinary matter; it is an invaluable blessing. When this steadfastness, this true determination, arises from deep within, you discover a center of strength and stability within yourself. It enables you to withstand the pressures and fluctuations of the outer world. The strongest wind cannot overturn such a mountain of steadfastness.

The poet-saint Mirabai entreats the Lord to dye her so completely with His love that she can withstand anything. She sings:

> O my beloved Krishna, dye my shawl
> in Your own color.
> Dye my being in Your own color.
> Dye my life in Your own color.
> I don't want it to be colored either red or yellow.
> Give my shawl a hue that is distinctly Your own.
> Dye my shawl in a permanent color,
> so that no matter how many times
> the washerman scrubs it,
> the color will not fade away.

Here, the washerman is the world. No matter how many struggles there are, how many distractions there are, still, O Lord, make this color very strong and let it be You.

> O Krishna, dye my shawl in Your own color.
> Unless you dye my shawl in Your own color,
> I am not going to go home.
> I am going to stay here forever.

> Mira says:
> My beloved Shri Krishna, the endearing One,
> the One who held the entire mountain
> on the tip of his little finger,
> Govardhana, my gaze is absorbed
> in the feet of the Lord.

> O my beloved Krishna, dye my shawl
>   in Your own color.
> Dye my heart in the hue of Your love.

MIRABAI IS DESCRIBING a profound inner state of longing that arises with the awakening of *kundalinī*. Many awe-inspiring experiences take place when this divine energy is awakened. A remarkable unfolding occurs within. You can never understand its mysteries in a way that satisfies the mind, that allows the mind to conjure up its favorite reasons and concepts. This unfolding is an alchemical process. It just happens. And when it does, you can watch it, you can learn to appreciate it, and ultimately you can become that beautiful experience.

Baba Muktananda gives explicit descriptions of this alchemical process in his spiritual autobiography *Play of Consciousness*. With great reverence and awe he speaks of the powerful meditation experiences that unfolded for him as part of the divine work of *kundalinī* awakening. For many meditators, however, the process of awakening is very subtle. Experiences occur based on each seeker's temperament, capacity, and knowledge. So don't worry about whether you are eligible for the intense experiences that Baba describes. Nor should you feel concerned and hope that these things *don't* happen to you. The *kundalinī shakti* is a supremely intelligent force. It will manifest only those things that are needed for your spiritual growth. Therefore, trust that the *kundalinī* knows perfectly what is right for you.

For example, you may have subtle experiences while you are chanting, because this practice purifies the chakras, the inner spiritual centers. If you have spent time chanting, you must have noticed how powerful it is, particularly after you have meditated. Recently during one of the programs, after meditation had concluded and everyone was chanting *Om Namah Shivāya*, I had a vision of mountain peaks filling the entire room. The sound of the chanting was emanating from the depths of the mountain and rising through the peaks into the heavens. Then the sound came back to all of us. It was so beautiful that I could have stayed and chanted for a long, long time.

Through spiritual practices like chanting, you become aware that the quality of steadfastness is growing within you. It is standing within you like a mountain. Then, no matter what you do and where you go, this strength is with you. You feel that your spine is very strong. You may feel that for the first time you have a backbone. You feel steadfast.

A Japanese sage once said, "Standing on the mountain, the entire world is within my knowing. In the crowded marketplace, I carry the mountain beneath my robe." Steadfastness is not just a mental creation. It is the steadiness of your innermost being.

The practice of hatha yoga also helps prepare the body to contain the nectar of steadfastness. When people practice hatha yoga earnestly, they experience a warm and gentle energy. It is like a wave of heat rising from the core of your being and spreading throughout the body. This warm energy supports and lubricates all the joints. It also confers a blanket of peace and great inner confidence. Depending on how deep your awareness goes during the postures, you will benefit accordingly. Hatha yoga is not about losing a few inches in your waist or shedding a few pounds. In the classical tradition of yoga, it is the inner attainment that matters.

Baba used to say that hatha yoga postures came from the meditation experiences of ancient sages. While they were meditating, their bodies would go through many contortions. And from these they developed the hatha yoga postures. It is our great good fortune that we now have these postures to stabilize the breath and strengthen our system so that the body can become a golden vehicle.

The truth is that everything in the outer world is impermanent. Looking wonderful on the outside evaporates with the passage of time. You age and the body changes. It is inevitable. But the attainment of inner greatness is strengthened with time and practice.

Be steadfast. Embrace your own inner courage. These qualities become yours only through the practices. There is no real shortcut on the journey to God.

ONCE A WOMAN HEARD about a heavenly mango. This divine food was said to impart all yogic attainments very quickly and to grant a person effortless meditation. Like many people in this modern age, the woman was looking for quick results, so she thought, "This is just what I need." She went around asking, "Have you heard about the heavenly mango? Do you know where it can be found?"

After many weeks, someone told her, "There is an ecstatic being called Shabir. Go to him. He has that very fruit."

"Where does he live?" she asked.

"Oh, he lives in a monastery in the desert."

It took her weeks to arrive at the monastery. As soon as she entered, she presented her request. "O Shabir, I hear you have the heavenly mango. Please give it to me right away!"

Shabir said, "Stay here. Do a little *japa* and chant."

"For how long?"

"As long as it takes," was the brief reply.

"I'm so busy. I don't really have time," she said, looking at her watch and checking her engagement diary. She left, convinced that this was not a place for her and thinking this man could really use some time-management skills.

Years went by, but wherever she went, whatever she did, she could not get the heavenly mango out of her mind. So out of frustration, she did a little *japa* and a little chanting. And sometimes she would even sit for meditation. Over time, she gave more and more of herself to spiritual practices. In this way, she prayed and meditated for thirty long years, always hoping that one day she would have the heavenly mango.

One auspicious day she met a very wise man. He saw her plight and told her, "I know who has the heavenly mango."

"You do?"

"Yes! Shabir."

"Shabir? The one who lives in a monastery in the desert?" Then she told him the whole story.

The wise man smiled at her and said, "Go to him and ask again."

Once again she set off. When she arrived at the monastery, her heart began to melt. Everything was sparkling. She didn't know whether it all looked so shiny because she was crying or because everything was amazingly exquisite. Her heart was gripped with ecstasy. Her whole being began to melt in the shimmering presence of the monastery. Finally, she made her way to Shabir. She knelt down and folded her hands, saying, "O Shabir, am I worthy enough to receive the celestial fruit?"

Much to her surprise, Shabir nodded his head and handed her the fruit.

As she held the mango, it seemed to be alive. It was breathing. It was luminous like the rising sun. Its aroma was intoxicating. To touch it was to touch heaven. To hold it was to be in heaven. She was ecstatic. And then, wistfully, she whispered, "Shabir, why didn't you give this to me when I came here the first time?"

Shabir smiled at her and very gently explained, "My good woman, when you first came, you had no time. You were in such a hurry. You couldn't stay even for a little while." And then he pointed to a tree and said, "This tree bears fruit every thirty years. You've done your sadhana. Thirty years have gone by. The mango is ripe and it's yours."

THE PURSUIT OF A LIFELONG PRACTICE requires the inspiration of steadfastness. Saint John of the Cross, the great Spanish mystic, says:

> Remember always that you came here for no other reason than to be a saint; thus, let nothing reign in your soul that does not lead you to sanctity.

Such steadfastness. You embrace your inner courage as you reach for the highest. You revere God's creation with the full knowledge that it is Consciousness. You move toward the inner world with total trust that you will find the hidden treasure. You dare to unravel the inner mystery. You give yourself the golden opportunity to become immersed in God's love.

There is an ancient Indian text called the *Tantrāloka*, which speaks about the powerful force that is unleashed as a seeker puts forth determined effort to be free. The *Tantrāloka* says:

> When a yogi is totally dedicated to removing the burden of his limited awareness, then the blazing energy of the divine shakti brings about the experience of the inner splendor of the supreme Consciousness that he seeks.

This blazing energy takes the form of benevolent grace. It is a form of the Guru's love. This blazing energy is the most beneficial force. It explodes from deep within the cavern of the heart. This is why once you receive shaktipat, you see everything sparkling. You see greater beauty in everything. You see things you never saw before.

The *Tantrāloka* says one must be utterly determined in one's resolve. This means being totally dedicated to overcoming bondage, the illusion of separation from God. That is the primal bondage—experiencing disconnection, disassociation from God. As you put forth self-effort, *kundalinī shakti* rises up to unite with that effort. When *kundalinī* energy is awakened and you do your practices, the energy and the practices meet, and then there is an explosion.

In everyday life you experience a similar phenomenon. When you truly appreciate what is happening in your life, you can feel how the sweet creative energy rises up to meet your needs. And then you can say, "God is with me. The universe is supporting me. God is behind me."

When you are able to call forth inner courage and live from that place in everything you do, you remain undaunted by passing difficulties. Your heart is protected when all your actions arise from the vast lake of steadfastness. Truly, the power of steadfastness and courage is phenomenal.

In *Play of Consciousness*, Baba Muktananda writes:

> Once I had seen that sphere of unmanifest Light, I lost all fear. This is the state of liberation from individual existence. Since then, my courage has increased a great deal, and I no longer know any fear. I am not afraid of anything. I never think about what is going to happen. I never worry about what somebody will do. The place of fear within me is destroyed. I have attained total fearlessness.[2]

For many people, just reading these words invokes fearlessness. Just hearing about Baba's fearlessness makes them feel strong. Baba's words make it very clear that by being persistent in your practice, you bring steadfastness into your life. By focusing on the profound strength within, you can embrace your own inner courage.

Remember, embracing your courage is being true to yourself. So watch your thoughts. Watch your speech. Watch your actions. Allow yourself to receive inspiration from the vast lake of steadfastness. Be steadfast and embrace your own inner courage. Become the mountain.

DECEMBER 28, 1997
Palm Springs, California

EPILOGUE

*May you go to sleep at night filled with the power of courage
and experience the sweet flavor of divine contentment.
May you wake up in the morning with courage
and experience the sweet flavor of divine contentment.
May you apply yourself to spiritual practices
with the enthusiasm of courage
and experience the sweet flavor of divine contentment.
May you devote yourself to your family duties
with the inspiration of courage
and experience the sweet flavor of divine contentment.
May you follow discipline in your life
with the strength of courage
and experience the sweet flavor of divine contentment.
May you rise to the needs of every moment with the light of courage
and experience the sweet flavor of divine contentment.
May you live the life of your dreams
with the energy of your inner courage
and become steeped in divine contentment.
May you fulfill the purpose of your birth
with the illumination of courage
and become steeped in divine contentment.
May you awaken to your inner courage
and become steeped in divine contentment.*

COPYRIGHT PERMISSIONS

WE GRATEFULLY ACKNOWLEDGE PERMISSION
to quote passages from the following sources:

GUIDE TO SANSKRIT PRONUNCIATION

For the reader's convenience, the Sanskrit and Hindi terms most frequently used in Siddha Yoga literature and courses appear throughout the text in roman type with simple transliteration. *Śaktipāta*, for instance, is shaktipat; *sādhana* is sadhana, and so on. For less frequently used Sanskrit words, the long vowels are marked in the text. The standard international transliteration for each Sanskrit term is given in the notes and in brackets for the glossary entries.

For readers not familiar with Sanskrit, the following is a guide for pronunciation.

Vowels and Diphthongs

Sanskrit vowels are categorized as either long or short. In English transliteration, the long vowels are marked with a bar above the letter and are pronounced twice as long as the short vowels. The letters *e* and *o* are always pronounced as long vowels.

Short:	Long:	
a as in c*u*p	*ā* as in c*a*lm	*ai* as in *ai*sle
i as in g*i*ve	*e* as in s*a*ve	*au* as in c*o*w
u as in f*u*ll	*ī* as in s*ee*n	*ū* as in sch*oo*l
	o as in kn*o*w	

Consonants

The main differences between Sanskrit and English pronunciation of consonants are in the aspirated and retroflexive letters.

The aspirated letters have a definite *h* sound. The Sanskrit letter *kh* is pronounced as in inkhorn; the *th* as in boathouse; the *ph* as in loophole.

The retroflexes are pronounced with the tip of the tongue touching the hard palate; *ṭ*, for instance, is pronounced as in ant; *ḍ* as in end.

The sibilants are *ś*, *ṣ*, and *s*. The *ś* is pronounced as *sh* but with the tongue touching the soft palate; the *ṣ* as *sh* with the tongue touching the hard palate; the *s* as in history.

Other distinctive consonants are these:

c as in *ch*urch	*ṃ* is a strong nasal
ñ as in ca*ny*on	*ḥ* is a strong aspiration
ṛ as in w*ri*tten	

For a detailed pronunciation guide, see
The Nectar of Chanting, published by SYDA Foundation.

NOTES

Epigraph

1. *Bhagavad Gītā* 11.40
   namaḥ purastād atha pṛṣṭhatas te namo'stu te sarvata eva sarva
   anantavīryāmitavikramas tvaṃ sarvaṃ samāpnoṣi tato'si sarvaḥ

2. *Kulārṇava Tantra* 9.37
   na hī dhyānāt paro mantro na devas tvātmanaḥ paraḥ
   nānusandhānāt parā pūjā na hi tṛpteḥ paraṃ phalam
   English translation: M.P. Pandit, *Gems from the Tantras*
   (Pondicherry: All India Press, 1975).

1. Wake Up to Your Inner Courage and Become Steeped in Divine Contentment

1. Daniel Ladinsky, *I Heard God Laughing* (Walnut Creek, Calif.: Sufism Reoriented, 1996).
2. Swami Muktananda, "Cultivate the Self," *Siddha Path*, December, 1981.
3. John Balguy (1686-1748), British philosopher.
4. Swami Muktananda, *Sadgurunath Maharaj ki Jay*, 1975.
5. Swami Muktananda, *Conversations with Swami Muktananda* (South Fallsburg, N.Y.: SYDA Foundation, 1998).

How Does Fear Take Birth?

1. *Crest Jewel of Discrimination* 330
   yadā kadā vāpi vipaścid eṣa brahmaṇyanante'pyaṇumātrabhedam
   paśyathyathāmuṣya bhayaṃ tadaiva yad vikṣitam bhinnatyā pramādāt

2. Meditation and Happiness

1. Swami Muktananda, *Play of Consciousness* (South Fallsburg, N.Y.: SYDA Foundation, 1994).
2. Daniel Ladinsky, *I Heard God Laughing*.

3. Swami Muktananda, *From the Finite to the Infinite* (South Fallsburg, N.Y.: SYDA Foundation, 1994).

4. *Yajur Veda* 4.17
   eṣa te śukra tanūr etad varcas tayā sambhava bhrājam gaccha
   jūrasi dhṛtā manasā juṣṭā viṣṇave

5. *Uddhava Gītā* 9.45
   evaṃ samāhitamatiīr mām evātmānam ātmani
   vīcaṣṭe mayi sarvātman jyotirjyotiṣi samyutam
   English translation: Swami Madhavananda, *Uddhava Gītā* (Calcutta: Advaita Ashrama, 1971).

6. *Panchadashi* 9:153 by Swami Vidyaranya (14th century)
   yathā gādha-nidher labdhau nopāyaḥ khananaṃ vinā
   mal-lābhe'pi tathā svātmacintāṃ muktvā na cāparaḥ

7. Swami Muktananda, *Satsang with Baba*, Vol. 4 (Oakland, Calif.: SYDA Foundation, 1978).

8. *Katha Upanishad* 2.2.22
   aśarīraṃ śarireśv anavastheṣv avasthitam
   mahāntaṃ vibhūm ātmānaṃ matvā dhiro na śocati

9. Daniel Ladinsky, *I Heard God Laughing*.

3. Step Forward and Be the Light

1. Swami Muktananda, *Nothing Exists That Is Not Śiva* (South Fallsburg, N.Y.: SYDA Foundation, 1997).

2. *Avadhūta Stotram* 2,16
   nirvāsanaṃ nirsanaṃ nirakankṣaṃ sarvadoṣa-vivarjitam
   nirālambaṃ nirātankaṃ nityānandaṃ namāyaham
   yoga-pūrṇam tapo-mūrtim prema-pūrṇaṃ sudar'sanam
   jñāna-pūrṇaṃ kṛpā-mūrtiṃ nityānandaṃ namāyaham
   The Nectar of Chanting (South Fallsburg, N.Y.: SYDA Foundation, 1994).

3. Swami Muktananda, "Wherever You Are, Attain God," *Siddha Yoga*, March 1981, Vol. 9, No. 3.

4. The Courage to Know Your Own Worthiness

1. *Bhagavad Gita* 4.8
   paritrāṇāya sādhūnaṃ vināśāya ca duṣkṛtām
   dharmasaṃsthāpanārthāya saṃbhavāmi yuge yuge

2. *Bhagavad Gita* 4.7
yadā yadā hi dharmasya glānir bhavati bhārata
abhyutthānam adharmasya tadā tmānaṁ sṛjamyaham

5. The Steadiness of God's Presence

1. *Atharva Veda* 19.15.6
abhyaṁ mitrād a bhayam amitrād a bhayam jñātad abhayaṁ puro yaḥ
abhyam naktam abhayam divā naḥ sarvā āśā mama mitram bhavantu
English translation: Raimundo Panikkar, *The Vedic Experience*
Mantramanjari (London: Darton, Longman & Todd Ltd., 1977).

2. Swami Muktananda, *Swami Muktananda Paramahansa in Australia* (Melbourne, Australia, Shree Gurudev Meditation Centre, 1970).

3. Swami Muktananda, *Satsang with Baba* Vol. I (Oakland, Calif.: SYDA Foundation, 1974).

6. Let Your Heart Sing

1. *Rig Veda* 10.68.1
udapruto na vayo rakṣamāṇa vavadato abhriyasyeva ghoṣāḥ
giribhrajo normayo mandanto bṛhaspatim abhyarkā anāvan
English translation: Raimundo Panikkar, *The Vedic Experience*
Mantramanjarī (London: Darton, Longman &Todd Ltd., 1977).

2. Swami Muktananda, "The Mystery of an All Night Chant," *Baba Company*, January 1981.

3. Swami Muktananda, "Magnet of Divine Vibrations," *Baba Company*, January 1981.

7. Moving Out of the House of Lacks

1. *Vairagya-śatakam* 63
etasmād viramendriyārthagahanād āyāsakād āśraya
śreyomārgam aśes duḥkhaśama navyāpārad akṣaṁ kṣhaṇāt
svātmi bhāvam upaihi saṁtyaja nijām kallolalolaṁ gatiṁ
mābhūyo bhaja bhaṅgurām bhavaratim cetaḥ prasīdādhunā

2. Swami Muktananda, *I Have Become Alive* (South Fallsburg, N.Y.: SYDA Foundation, 1995).

3. Swami Muktananda, *From the Finite to the Infinite*.

4. Swami Muktananda, *From the Finite to the Infinite*.

8. Be Steadfast, Embrace Your Own Inner Courage

1. Swami Muktananda, *From the Finite to the Infinite*.
2. Stephen Clissold, editor, *The Wisdom of Spanish Mystics* (New York: New Direction Books, 1977).
3. *Jñāneshvari* 18.858
   Swami Kripananda, *Jnaneshwar's Gita* (South Fallsburg, N.Y.: SYDA Foundation, 1999).
4. Swami Muktananda, "Address at Simla," *Shree Gurudev Ashram Newsletter*, June 1973.

9. A Mountain of Steadiness

1. Swami Muktananda, *Secret of the Siddhas* (South Fallsburg, N.Y.: SYDA Foundation, 1994).
2. Swami Muktananda, *Play of Consciousness*.

GLOSSARY

ABSOLUTE, THE
The highest Reality; supreme Consciousness; the pure, untainted, changeless Truth.

AKBAR
(1542-1605) A great Moghul emperor who consolidated an extensive Indian empire. His administrative skills, benevolent nature, and interest in culture and religion endeared him to his people.

AKKAMAHADEVI
An ecstatic twelfth-century poet-saint of South India. In her short life she composed many devotional poems in the Kannada language.

ANTARSTHITI [antarsthiti]
The inner state of steadfastness.

ARATI [āratī]
1) A ritual act of worship during which a flame, symbolic of the individual soul, is waved before the form of a deity, sacred being, or image that embodies the light of Consciousness. 2) The name of the morning and evening prayer that is sung with the waving of lights, in honor of Bhagawan Nityananda, twice each day in Siddha Yoga meditation ashrams.

ARJUNA
One of the heroes of the Indian epic *Mahābhārata*, known for his valor and considered to be the greatest warrior of all. He was the friend and devotee of Lord Krishna, who revealed the teachings of the *Bhagavad Gītā* to him on the battlefield.

ASHRAM [āśrama]
The dwelling place of a Guru or saint; a monastic retreat site where seekers engage in spiritual practices and study the sacred teachings of yoga.

ATHARVA VEDA [atharvaveda]
One of the four fundamental scriptures of India; it consists of prayers for the healing of disease and the restoration of harmony in the world, and songs celebrating the power and omniscience of God. *See also* VEDAS.

AVADHUTA STOTRAM [avadhūta stotram]
(*avadhūta*, an enlightened being) A hymn chanted in Siddha Yoga meditation ashrams in praise of the great Siddha Bhagawan Nityananda.

BABA [bābā]
A term of affection and respect for a saint or holy man. *See also* MUKTANANDA, SWAMI.

BABA MUKTANANDA
See MUKTANANDA, SWAMI.

BADE BABA
(*lit.*, elder father) An affectionate name for Bhagawan Nityananda, Swami Muktananda's Guru. *See also* NITYANANDA, BHAGAWAN.

BHAGAVAD GITA [*bhagavadgītā*]

(*lit.*, song of God) One of the world's spiritual treasures and an essential scripture of Hinduism; a portion of the *Mahābhārata* in which Lord Krishna instructs his disciple Arjuna on the nature of the universe, God, and the supreme Self.

BHAGAWAN NITYANANDA

See NITYANANDA, BHAGAWAN.

BHAJAN [*bhajana*]

A Hindi devotional song in praise of God.

BIRBAL

(1528-1586) An inspired philosopher, poet, and wit who was the friend and prime minister of King Akbar.

BLUE PEARL

A brilliant blue light, the size of a tiny seed, which can be seen in meditation; the subtle abode of the inner Self.

BRAHMACHARYA [*brahmacārya*]

(*lit.*, abiding in Brahman, the Absolute) The practice of continence and chastity for the purpose of spiritual discipline.

BRAHMAN [*brahman*]

The Vedic term for the absolute Reality, supreme Consciousness.

CONSCIOUSNESS

The intelligent, supremely independent, divine Energy, which creates, pervades, and supports the entire universe.

DARSHAN [*darśana*]

(*lit.*, to have sight of; viewing) A glimpse or vision of a saint; being in the presence of a holy person; seeing God or an image of God.

DHARANA [*dhāraṇā*]

A centering technique, a spiritual exercise that leads one to the experience of God within.

DHARMIC

In accordance with righteousness, or dharma.

EGO

In yoga, the limited sense of "I" that is identified with the body, mind, and senses; sometimes described as "the veil of suffering."

GOVARDHANA

A name of Lord Krishna, based on the legend that he lifted the mountain Govardhana like an umbrella to protect his village from heavy rains sent by the wrath of the god Indra.

GOVINDA, GOPALA

Names for Lord Krishna, signifying mastery of the senses and the mind.

GURU [*guru*]

(*lit.*, teacher) A spiritual master who lives in the constant experience of the divine inner Self and who is able both to initiate seekers and to guide them on the spiritual path to liberation. A true Guru is required to be learned in the scriptures and must belong to a lineage of masters. *See also* SHAKTIPAT; SIDDHA.

GURUDEV SIDDHA PEETH

The mother ashram of Siddha Yoga meditation, located in Ganeshpuri, India.

GURU GITA [*gurugītā*]

(*lit.*, song of the Guru) A sacred text consisting of mantras that describe the nature of the Guru, the Guru-

disciple relationship, and techniques
of meditation on the Guru. In Siddha
Yoga meditation ashrams, the *Guru
Gītā* is chanted every morning.

HAFIZ

(1326-1390) A Sufi from Persia who
was a court poet and professor.
Originally known as Shams-uddin
Muhammed, he chose Hafiz ("mem-
orizer") as a pen name; it designates
one who knows the *Qur'an* by heart.

HATHA YOGA [*haṭhayoga*]

Yogic practices, both physical and
mental, performed for the purpose of
purifying and strengthening the physical and subtle bodies. *See also* YOGA.

JAPA [*japa*]

(*lit.*, prayer uttered in a low voice)
Repetition of a mantra, either
silently or aloud. *See also* MANTRA.

JNANESHWAR MAHARAJ

(1275-1296) Foremost among the poet-
saints of Maharashtra. The *Jñāneshvarī*,
his verse commentary written in the
Marathi language on the *Bhagavad
Gītā*, is acknowledged as one of the
world's most important spiritual
works. *See also* BHAGAVAD GITA.

KARMA [*karma*]

(*lit.*, action) 1) Any action—physical, verbal, or mental. 2) Destiny,
which is caused by past actions,
mainly those of previous lives.

KRISHNA

(*lit.*, the dark one) The eighth incar-
nation of Lord Vishnu. Called "the
dark one" because of the dark blue
color of his skin, his spiritual teachings are contained in the *Bhagavad
Gītā*. *See also* BHAGAVAD GITA.

KULARNAVA TANTRA [*kulārṇavatantra*]

An ancient treatise on the Guru, the
disciple, the mantra, and many tra-
ditional practices of worship.

KUNDALINI [*kuṇḍalinī*]

(*lit.*, coiled one) The supreme power;
the primordial energy (shakti) that
lies coiled at the base of the spine.
Through the descent of grace (shaktipat), this extremely subtle force, also
described as the supreme Goddess,
is awakened and begins to purify the
entire being. As Kundalini travels
upward through the central channel,
She pierces the various chakras, finally
reaching the *sahasrāra* at the crown
of the head. There, the individual
self merges into the supreme Self
and attains the state of God-realization. *See also* SHAKTI; SHAKTIPAT.

MANTRA [*mantra*]

Sacred words or divine sounds
invested with the power to protect,
purify, and transform the individual
who repeats them; the names of God.
See also OM NAMAH SHIVAYA.

MIRA, MIRABAI

A sixteenth-century Rajasthani queen
and poet-saint; out of devotion for
Lord Krishna, she left the palace
to wander from village to village,
singing of His glory.

MUKTANANDA, SWAMI

(1908-1982) A Siddha of the modern
age; Gurumayi Chidvilasananda's
Guru, often referred to as Baba.
This great yogi brought the powerful and rare initiation known as
shaktipat to the West at the command of his own Guru, Bhagawan
Nityananda.

MURTI [*mūrti*]
(*lit.*, embodiment; figure; image) A representation of God or of a deity that has been sanctified and enlivened by worship.

NACHIKETA
One of the principal characters of the *Katha Upanishad*. When he was offered a boon by Yama, the lord of death, he asked for the supreme knowledge of the Absolute. *See also* UPANISHADS.

NASRUDDIN, SHEIKH
A figure originating in Turkish folklore during the Middle Ages, used by spiritual teachers to illustrate the antics of the human mind.

NERI, PHILLIP
(1515-1595) Italian priest and mystic who attracted disciples from all walks of life and helped to renew the religious life of Rome.

NITYANANDA, BHAGAWAN
(d. 1961) A great Siddha master, Swami Muktananda's Guru, also known as Bade Baba ("elder" Baba). He was a born Siddha, living his entire life in the highest state of consciousness. In both Gurudev Siddha Peeth in Ganeshpuri, India, and Shree Muktananda Ashram in South Fallsburg, New York, Swami Muktananda has dedicated a temple of meditation to honor Bhagawan Nityananda.

OM NAMAH SHIVAYA
[*oṃ namaḥ śivāya*]
(*lit.*, *Om*, salutations to Shiva) The Sanskrit mantra of the Siddha Yoga lineage; known as the great redeeming mantra because of its power to grant both worldly fulfillment and spiritual realization. *Om* is the primordial sound; *Namah* is to honor or bow to; *Shivāya* denotes divine Consciousness, the Lord who dwells in every heart.

RASA [*rasa*]
1) Flavor, taste. 2) A subtle energy of richness, sweetness, and delight.

RIG VEDA [*ṛgveda*]
The oldest of the four Vedas, the *Rig Veda* is composed of more than a thousand hymns, including those that invoke the gods of the fire rituals. *See also* VEDAS.

SACCHIDANANDA [*saccidānanda*]
(*lit.*, absolute existence, consciousness, and bliss) In Vedantic philosophy, the three indivisible qualities of the Absolute.

SADGURU [*sadguru*]
See GURU.

SADHANA [*sādhana*]
1) A spiritual discipline or path. 2) Practices, both physical and mental, on the spiritual path.

SAMADHI [*samādhi*]
The state of meditative union with the Absolute.

SAMA VEDA [*sāmaveda*]
One of the four Vedas, the *Sāma Veda* is a collection of hymns sung to melodies of great beauty. *See also* VEDAS.

SANNYASA [*sannyāsa*]
1) Monkhood. 2) The ceremony and vows of monkhood.

SARASWATI [*sarasvatī*]
The goddess of speech, learning, and the arts.

SATSANG [*satsaṅga*]
(*lit.*, the company of the Truth) The company of saints and devotees; a gathering of devotees for the purpose of chanting, meditation, and listening to scriptural teachings or readings.

SELF
Divine Consciousness residing in the individual, described as the witness of the mind or the pure I-awareness.

SEVA [*sevā*]
(*lit.*, service) Selfless service; work offered to God, performed without attachment and with the attitude that one is not the doer. In Siddha Yoga meditation ashrams, *sevā* is a spiritual practice, and students seek to perform all of their actions in this spirit of selfless offering.

SHAKTI [*śakti*]
The divine Mother, dynamic spiritual energy; the creative force of the universe. *See also* KUNDALINI.

SHAKTIPAT [*śaktipāta*]
(*lit.*, descent of grace) Yogic initiation in which the Siddha Guru transmits his fully awakened spiritual energy into the aspirant, thereby awakening the aspirant's dormant *kundalinī*. *See also* GURU; KUNDALINI.

SHANKARACHARYA
(788-820) One of the most celebrated of India's philosophers and sages, he traveled throughout the country expounding the philosophy of Advaita ("nondual") Vedanta. Among his many works is *Viveka Chūḍāmani*, "The Crest Jewel of Discrimination."

SHREE MUKTANANDA ASHRAM
The Siddha Yoga meditation ashram in South Fallsburg, New York, established in 1979 as the international headquarters of SYDA Foundation, the nonprofit organization that administers Siddha Yoga programs and publications. *See also* ASHRAM.

SHRI [*śrī*]
A term of respect that means "wealth, prosperity, glory, and success," and signifies mastery of all these.

SIDDHA [*siddha*]
An enlightened yogi; one who lives in the state of unity-consciousness; one whose experience of the supreme Self is uninterrupted and whose identification with the ego has been dissolved.

SIDDHA YOGA [*siddhayoga*]
(*lit.*, the yoga of perfection) A path to union of the individual and the Divine that begins with shaktipat, the inner awakening by the grace of a Siddha Guru. Siddha Yoga is the name Swami Muktananda gave to this path, which he first brought to the West in 1970; Swami Chidvilasananda is the living master of this lineage. *See also* GURU; KUNDALINI; SHAKTIPAT.

SWAMI
A respectful term of address for a *sannyāsi* or monk.

TANTRALOKA [*tantrāloka*]
An encyclopedic work by the eleventh-century sage Abhinavagupta, explicating the Shaiva philosophy and practices in all their aspects.

TAPASYA [*tapasyā*]
(*lit.*, heat) 1) Austerities. 2) The fire

of yoga; the heat generated by spiritual practices.

TEMPLE

Unless it is otherwise specified, "the Temple" refers to the Bhagawan Nityananda Temple at Gurudev Siddha Peeth in Ganeshpuri, India, or at Shree Muktananda Ashram in South Fallsburg, New York.

TUKADYADAS

(20th century) A poet-saint from Maharashtra, India; a contemporary and friend of Swami Muktananda. During the days of Muktananda's sadhana, the two great yogis often chanted together the many *bhajans*, or devotional songs, that Tukadyadas composed about the spiritual path and devotion to the Guru.

UDDHAVA GITA [*uddhavagītā*]

A section of the *Shrīmad Bhāgavatam* in which Lord Krishna, on the eve of his departure from the world, gives his parting instructions to his beloved disciple Uddhava.

UPANISHADS [*upaniṣad*]

(*lit.*, sitting close to; secret teachings) The inspired teachings, visions, and mystical experiences of the ancient sages of India. With immense variety of form and style, all of these scriptures (exceeding one hundred texts) give the same essential teaching—that the individual soul and God are one. *See also* VEDAS.

VEDAS [*veda*]

(*lit.*, knowledge) Among the most ancient, revered, and sacred of the world's scriptures, the four Vedas are regarded as divinely revealed, eternal wisdom. They are the *Rig Veda, Atharva Veda, Sāma Veda,* and *Yajur Veda.*

VINA [*vīṇā*]

A stringed musical instrument sacred to Shri Saraswati, the goddess of the arts and learning.

VIVEKA CHUDAMANI [*vivekacūḍāmaṇi*]

(*lit.*, the crest jewel of discrimination) An eighth-century philosophical commentary on Advaita Vedanta written by Shankaracharya; it expounds the teaching that only Brahman, the Absolute, is real. *See also* SHANKARACHARYA.

YAJUR VEDA [*yajurveda*]

A scripture whose hymns specify sacrificial formulas and rites and the rules for their correct performance, which are said to control the harmonious functioning of the universe. *See also* VEDAS.

YOGA [*yoga*]

(*lit.*, union) The spiritual practices and disciplines that lead a seeker to evenness of mind, to the severing of the union with pain, and, through detachment, to skill in action. Ultimately, the path of yoga leads to the constant experience of the Self.

INDEX

ABOUT GURUMAYI CHIDVILASANANDA

GURUMAYI CHIDVILASANANDA is a spiritual teacher in the ancient yogic tradition of India. As the head of a lineage of meditation masters, she continues the time-honored role of sages in every tradition—helping seekers awaken to their own inner greatness and to the divinity inherent in the universe. Gurumayi follows in the footsteps of her spiritual master, Swami Muktananda, who brought the teachings and practices of the path of Siddha Yoga meditation to the West in the 1970s, in what he called a "meditation revolution." Before he passed away in 1982, he selected Gurumayi as his successor and ordained her as a swami, a monk in the Saraswati order. Swami Muktananda was himself the successor to Bhagawan Nityananda, a much-revered saint of modern India.

Gurumayi travels widely, taking the teachings and practices of this path to seekers in many countries. She has conducted thousands of programs in cities around the world, as well as in the two major Siddha Yoga retreat centers: Shree Muktananda Ashram in South Fallsburg, New York, and Gurudev Siddha Peeth in Ganeshpuri, Maharashtra, India.

Gurumayi's work encompasses a charitable organization, The PRASAD Project, that assists people in need in several countries with medical, dental, and community self-help projects.

SWAMI MUKTANANDA'S GURU, BHAGAWAN NITYANANDA

GURUMAYI'S GURU, SWAMI MUKTANANDA

Wherever she travels, whatever form her work takes, her focus remains the same. Gurumayi calls on people everywhere to wake up to their inner strength and to put into action the natural joy that abounds in their hearts. "The light of the truth is infinite," says Gurumayi, "and this infinite light must definitely be translated into everyday life."

FURTHER READING
PUBLISHED BY SYDA FOUNDATION

by

Gurumayi Chidvilasananda

ENTHUSIASM

"Be filled with enthusiasm and sing God's glory" is the theme of this collection of talks by Gurumayi. In these pages, she inspires us to let the radiance of enthusiasm shine through every action, every thought, every minute of our lives. This, Gurumayi says, is singing God's glory.

THE YOGA OF DISCIPLINE

"From the standpoint of the spiritual path," Gurumayi says, "the term *discipline* is alive with the joyful expectancy of divine fulfillment." In this series of talks on cultivating discipline of the wandering senses, Gurumayi shows us how this practice brings great joy.

REMEMBRANCE

Gurumayi draws our attention to the great things in our lives that are worth remembering: our own innate goodness, our worthiness to give and receive love, and the extraordinary blessings that flow through our lives.

MY LORD LOVES A PURE HEART:
THE YOGA OF DIVINE VIRTUES

Fearlessness, reverence, compassion, freedom from anger—Gurumayi describes how these magnificent virtues are an integral part of our true nature. The list of virtues introduced is based on chapter 16 of the *Bhagavad Gītā*.

Poetry and Contemplation

SMILE, SMILE, SMILE!

Throughout the ages, great spiritual masters have offered their teachings in spontaneous outpourings of poetry. In these poems, Gurumayi demonstrates the mystical process of spiritual contemplation, offering the reader a deeper awareness of the perfection of the soul. (Also available on audio cassette, read by the author.)

ASHES AT MY GURU'S FEET

In this priceless collection of her poetry, offered to her Guru, Swami Muktananda, Gurumayi generously shares with us her own experience of the spiritual path. In the universal language of poetry, Gurumayi portrays how the path of love for the Guru can draw the fire of grace and open the disciple to purest light. *Illustrated.*

THE MAGIC OF THE HEART: REFLECTIONS ON DIVINE LOVE

In these profound and tender reflections on divine love, Gurumayi makes it clear that the supreme Heart is a place we must get to know. It is here, she tells us, in the interior of the soul, that "the Lord reveals Himself every second of the day."

RESONATE WITH STILLNESS

Daily Contemplations by Swami Muktananda, Swami Chidvilasananda

Every sentence of this exquisite collection of contemplations is an expression of wisdom and love from the Siddha Yoga masters. The selections are arranged around twelve themes of spiritual life, with a contemplation for each day of the year.

Further Reading

by

Swami Muktananda

PLAY OF CONSCIOUSNESS

In this intimate and powerful portrait, Swami Muktananda describes his own journey to Self-realization, revealing the process of transformation he experienced under the guidance of his Guru, Bhagawan Nityananda.

FROM THE FINITE TO THE INFINITE

This compilation of questions and answers is drawn from Baba Muktananda's travels in the West. In it, Baba addresses all the issues a seeker might encounter on the spiritual path, from the earliest days to the culmination of the journey.

WHERE ARE YOU GOING?

A comprehensive introduction to the teachings of Siddha Yoga meditation, this lively and anecdotal book explores the nature of the mind, the Self, and the inner power, as well as mantra, meditation, and the Guru.

I HAVE BECOME ALIVE

Here Baba shows us how to integrate the inner quest with the demands of contemporary life. He illumines such topics as spiritual discipline, the ego, marriage, parenting, experiencing love, and attaining God while embracing the world.

Library of Congress Cataloging-in-Publication Data.
Chidvilasananda, Gurumayi.
    Courage and contentment : a collection of talks on spiritual life /
Gurumayi Chidvilasananda.
        p.   cm.
    Includes index.
    ISBN 0-911307-77-x (pbk.)
    1. Spiritual life.   2. Siddha yoga (Trademark)   1. Title.
BP610.C45   1999
299'.93—dc21

                                                99-23685
                                                   CIP

183

You may learn more about the teachings and practices
of Siddha Yoga meditation by contacting

SYDA FOUNDATION
PO BOX 600, 371 BRICKMAN RD
SOUTH FALLSBURG, NY 12779-0600, USA

TEL: 914-434-2000

or

GURUDEV SIDDHA PEETH
PO GANESHPURI, PIN 401 206
DISTRICT THANA, MAHARASHTRA, INDIA

Please visit our website at www.siddhayoga.org

For further information on books in print by Swami Muktananda and
Gurumayi Chidvilasananda, editions in translation, and audio
and video recordings, please contact

SIDDHA YOGA MEDITATION BOOKSTORE
PO BOX 600, 371 BRICKMAN RD
SOUTH FALLSBURG, NY 12779-0600, USA

TEL: 914-434-2000 EXT. 1700

Call toll-free from the United States and Canada: 888-422-3334
Fax toll-free from the United States and Canada: 888-422-3339